FOREWORD BY **P. DAVID PEARSON**

The Truth About

DIBELS

What It Is

What It Does

KENNETH S. GOODMAN

with

Alan Flurkey | Tsuguhiko Kato | Constance Kamii
Maryann Manning | Susan Seay | Catherine Thome
Robert J. Tierney | Sandra Wilde

HEINEMANN
Portsmouth, NH

Heinemann
A division of Reed Elsevier Inc.
361 Hanover Street
Portsmouth, NH 03801–3912
www.heinemann.com

Offices and agents throughout the world

A previous edition of this book, titled *Examining DIBELS: What It Is and What
It Does*, was published by the Vermont Society for the Study of Education.

Published in cooperation with the Vermont Society for the Study of
Education (VSSE) and the Center for the Expansion of Language and
Thinking (CELT).

Library of Congress Cataloging-in-Publication Data
The truth about DIBELS : what it is, what it does / edited by Kenneth S.
Goodman ; foreword by P. David Pearson.
    p. cm.
  Includes bibliographical references.
  ISBN-13: 978-0-325-01050-2
  ISBN-10: 0-325-01050-1 (pbk. : alk. paper)
  1. Reading (Primary)—Ability testing—United States.   2. Educational
tests and measurements—United States—Evaluation.   I. Goodman,
Kenneth S.

LB1525.75.T78 2006
372.48—dc22   2006014782

Acquisitions editor: Lois Bridges
Editor: Gloria Pipkin
Production: Lynne Costa
Cover design: Night & Day Design
Typesetter: House of Equations, Inc.
Manufacturing: Louise Richardson

Printed in the United States of America on acid-free paper
10   09   08   07   06   VP   2   3   4   5

Contents

Foreword

P. David Pearson

*W*hen it comes to controversial issues in the teaching of reading, I have built a reputation for taking positions characterized as situated in "the radical middle" (Pearson, 2001)—not too conservative, not too liberal, just right (or at least I like to think so!). Not so on DIBELS. I have decided to join that group of scholars and teachers and parents who are convinced that DIBELS is the worst thing to happen to the teaching of reading since the development of flash cards.

I take this extreme position for a single reason—DIBELS shapes instruction in ways that are bad for students (they end up engaging in curricular activities that do not promote their progress as readers) and bad for teachers (it requires them to judge student progress and shape instruction based on criteria that are not consistent with our best knowledge about the nature of reading development).

The appeal of DIBELS. So if a group of eminent scholars such as those represented in this volume thinks DIBELS is so terrible, so malevolent, and so harmful, then why is it so popular? Why is it used in so many states, districts, and schools? Several reasons come readily to mind—some technical, some curricular, and some political in origin.

First, DIBELS has tremendous scientific cachet. If you go onto the DIBELS website, you find yourself awash in a sea of numbers—reliability indices, validity indicators, the number of students currently using DIBELS (almost 2,000,000 at the latest count). I have included a few of the more important ones in Table 1, which I extracted from the publicly accessible data on the website (http://dibels.uoregon.edu).

Table 1: *Psychometric characteristics of DIBELS*

	Alternate Form Reliability	Criterion-related Validity	
Letter Name Fluency	.88	Concurrent Validity WJ: .70	Predictive Validity .65–.71
Initial Sound Fluency	.72	DPSF: .48 WJ Readiness: .36	CBM: .45 WJ Reading: .36
Phoneme Segmentation Fluency	.79	WJ Readiness: .54	DNWF: .62 WJ Reading: .68
Nonsense Word Fluency	.83	WJ Readiness: .59	CBM: .60–.82 WJ Reading: .66
Oral Reading Fluency	.89–.94*	.52–.91*	
Retell Fluency	.59: ORF*		

KEY: WJ — Woodcock-Johnson
     CBM — Curriculum-Based Measures
     DPSF — DIBELS Phonemic Segmentation Fluency
     DNWF — DIBELS Nonsense Word Fluency

*The estimates for the reliability and validity of the ORF approach are based upon older studies documenting the general approach of Curriculum-Based Measures (Good & Jefferson, 1998; Tindal, Marston, & Deno, 1983) as cited on the DIBELS website (Good & Kaminski, 2002), not on the specific passages included in DIBELS.

From a psychometric perspective, the reliability data are impressive, especially for individually administered tests requiring human judgments about response correctness. One can trust the scores to be stable, at least in the short run (see Paris, 2005). And the validity indicators tell us how much these tests are similar to other tests of reading and verbal ability. I have divided the construct of criterion-related validity into two categories: (a) *concurrent* (how well does a given subtest correlate with scores on a test given at the same time as the subtest?) and (b) *predictive* (how well does a subtest predict scores on a test given at some point in the future?). What can be said of these correlations is that they are roughly of the same magnitude that we find among a wide range of measures of reading and verbal measures (see Paris, 2005, for an account of these patterns of covariation). It is interesting to note that the psychometric data for the Oral Reading Fluency and Retelling measures are based on the assumption that evidence about the general pool of Curriculum-Based Measures of which the DIBELS passages are a part will suffice as a measure of their psychometric rigor. On this matter, it is important to note that in a recent independent study of the predictive validity of DIBELS Oral Reading Fluency (given in Grade 3 and used to predict end of the year scores on the Terra Nova standardized reading test), Pressley et al. (2005) concluded that ". . . DIBELS mis-predicts reading performance on other assessments much of the time, and at best is a measure of who reads quickly without regard to whether the reader comprehends what is read."

Another reason for the appeal of DIBELS is its transparent match with the sort of curriculum championed by the Reading First plank of No Child Left Behind (2002). This association links DIBELS to another "scientific" indicator, the National Reading Panel (NRP) report (2000) by virtue of the fact that the NRP report serves as the research architecture for Reading First. There can be no doubt that the NRP's "big five" (phonemic awareness, phonics, fluency, vocabulary, and comprehension) shape instruction in schools with Reading First grants, and by extension, in *all* schools (because states, quite understandably, want to ensure alignment to NCLB/RF, and the scientific aura that comes with it, for all their schools, not just the ones eligible for extra funding).[1] It is also interesting to note that

---

[1] While it goes beyond the scope of this essay, it is important to note that there is nothing magical about the focus on this particular set of "big five" components of reading. The impact of writing or oral language development on reading, grouping, text difficulty, talk about text, and opportunity to read are just as important a set of curricular components as are the current big five, but they did not surface in the NRP report (2000), either because the body of experimental research undergirding them was insufficient to permit either meta-analysis of the sort championed by the panel or because these issues lay outside the boundaries of the individual and

DIBELS is available in conjunction with certain commercial programs; for example, Scott-Foresman (in the spirit of full disclosure, the company with which I serve as a basal author) markets DIBELS alongside of its reading program for elementary kids. This sort of juxtaposition only increases its transparent connection to curriculum.

The third reason for DIBELS' appeal is simplicity and ease of use. Imagine getting important information for monitoring student progress with one-minute samples of performance. Not only how many words read correctly in a minute, but rates for every possible behavior: letters named per minute, phonemes identified per minute, words named per minute, words recalled from a passage in a minute. Contrast the ease and simplicity of DIBELS with the exhortations of nuance and complexity one gets with the detailed analysis of oral reading one gets from running records or miscue analysis or from schemes for understanding students' retelling. It is easy to see how and why a busy teacher, overwhelmed with the responsibilities of planning instruction for students with many needs and meeting the requirements of bureaucratic reporting systems, might opt for the efficiency of DIBELS.

The fourth plank of DIBELS' appeal is based on its political positioning in the enactment of NCLB and Reading First policy. Evidence providing direct links between the advice or mandate of federal officials and the tools chosen by various states as the official scientifically based assessment portfolio for their Reading First implementations is always difficult to document (but see *Education Week*, September 7, 2005; Manning, Kamii, & Kato, this volume; Manzo, *Education Week*, September 28, 2005, for reports of such influence). Nonetheless, the ubiquity of DIBELS

---

collective interests of the panel members (Samuels, 2006). Researchers have no responsibility, in principle, to ensure that all aspects of a full reading curriculum are addressed in such a review. For better or worse (probably better) teachers and schools do. They have to decide what texts kids should read even though the research on optimal text types or combinations thereof do not permit a definitive conclusion about what kids should read. The danger, of course, with a document like the NRP is that the education profession will be seduced into believing, even though the NRP never intended so, that the big five is *all* that schools and teachers need to worry about. Even a cursory examination of state standards and state programs to guide the use of Reading First funds would suggest that the narrow view of curriculum promoted by the big five is real, not imaginary.

as the "preferred" progress monitoring tool across various states gives one pause to wonder whether informal coaching, in some cases out and out insistence on the part of federal officials or reviewers (Manning, Kamii, & Kato, this volume) to move in the direction of DIBELS, did not play a more important role than natural market forces in creating the obvious competitive advantage it holds (*Education Week*, September 7, 2005; Manzo, *Education Week*, September 28, 2005). Of course, it does not hurt that DIBELS was officially blessed as a "scientifically valid" instrument for purposes of progress monitoring by the Reading First Assessment Academy (http://idea.uoregon.edu/assessment/index.html), an advisory group on which DIBELS author Roland Good served. It seems to me that federal officials, at a minimum, are ethically and professionally obligated to explain the widespread use of DIBELS (especially in a marketplace flooded with potential competitors) and the apparent conflict of interest that seems to occur in this situation. I would even appreciate it if someone had the courage to 'fess up what seems, on the face of it, to be such an obvious conclusion—that privilege and favoritism, not merit, are behind this unlikely dominance of DIBELS across such a wide range of states.

The Problem with DIBELS

So what is the problem with DIBELS? Why am I, and why are so many other scholars, so concerned about its widespread and ever-increasing use? The answer to this question is, of course, what this book is all about. In the anchor paper in this book, Ken Goodman argues convincingly that DIBELS is much more than a test—that it has, de facto, become an implicit (perhaps even an explicit) blueprint for a curriculum—driving publishers, district officials, principals, and teachers into a narrow curricular mode in which only the big five (and mostly the even bigger three of phonics, phonemic awareness, and fluency) are taught at the expense of other curricular foci. The cost, in terms of human frustration and curricular opportunity, Goodman argues, is serious.

The other papers in this volume—by Tierney and Thome on its broad policy influence; by Seay on its failure to deliver its promise of increased achievement to Alabama; and Manning, Kamii, and Kato on its concurrent validity—all make related points about DIBELS. Interestingly, all either assume or draw similar conclusions about DIBELS' capacity to shape instruction in counterproductive ways by directing schools and teachers to a limited set of features of the reading curriculum. Most directly on point is the paper by Tierney and Thome, in which they point out the costs that schools, teachers, and students must bear when means are confused with ends. Students are held accountable to the indicators rather than the outcomes of progress. Teachers are forced to shape instruction in ways that violate well-documented theories of development, to privilege some aspects of literate performance over others, and to value students' performance over their vitality and identity. More importantly, Tierney and Thome point out, in a stroke of irony, that teachers are forced to assume a professional disposition at odds with the document serving as the architecture for Reading First—the National Reading Panel report (Tierney & Thome, this volume, page 50).

Of course, the authors of DIBELS, and the Reading First Assessment Academy that blessed DIBELS, would argue that these stories of curricular influence represent misuses rather than valid uses of DIBELS. They would say that DIBELS is authorized for only one of four primary purposes of assessment, progress monitoring, and, as such, it should be used only as a "thermometer" to gauge student learning, not as a "vision" to guide specific instructional foci.[2] But one of the first statements one encounters on the DIBELS website (http://dibels.uoregon.edu/dibelsinfo.php) is this description of what they are and what they are good for:

> The Dynamic Indicators of Basic Early Literacy Skills (DIBELS) are a set of standardized, individually administered measures of

---

[2]The four purposes of assessment required in Reading First are (a) screening—determining who might need extra help, (b) progress monitoring—benchmark assessments administered at regular intervals to determine who is, and is not, on track, (c) diagnosis—determining specific needs of specific students to guide specific interventions, and (d) outcome assessment—judging the effectiveness of a program, intervention, curriculum, etc.

early literacy development. They are designed to be short (one minute) fluency measures used to regularly monitor the development of pre-reading and early reading skills.

The measures were developed upon the essential early literacy domains discussed in both the National Reading Panel (2000) and National Research Council (1998) reports to assess student development of phonological awareness, alphabetic understanding, and automaticity and fluency with the code. Each measure has been thoroughly researched and demonstrated to be reliable and valid indicators of early literacy development and predictive of later reading proficiency to aid in the early identification of students who are not progressing as expected. When used as recommended, the results can be used to evaluate individual student development as well as provide grade-level feedback toward validated instructional objectives.

The major unknown in this formulation is, of course, what is done with the information provided to fulfill the goal of the last sentence: ". . . to evaluate individual student development as well as provide grade-level feedback toward validated instructional objectives." If the assumption is that teachers should teach and students should learn the skills measured by DIBELS, then these subtests do, in fact, become a curricular blueprint. One could imagine a parallel world in which they really were used as a thermometer—where a full and balanced curriculum was provided, and speed and fluency were regarded as the natural outcomes, not the objectives, of such a curriculum. My own view: in most (not all, but most) places in which it is used, DIBELS guides instruction right into the big five (and in lots of places the even bigger three), and all else (e.g., writing, oral language, disciplinary knowledge, discussion) has to compete for a very small piece of the curricular pie.

Of parallel importance, Goodman argues, is that DIBELS is based upon a flawed view of the nature of the reading process and, because of this fundamental flaw, provides all who use it with a misrepresentation of reading development. It digs too deeply into the infrastructure of reading skill and process and comes up with a lot of bits and pieces but not the orchestrated whole of reading as a skilled human process. Manning, Kamii, and Kato, in their chapter, provide correlational evidence to support this point, noting that the Phoneme Sound Segmentation Fluency test demonstrated only the most modest of correlations with a concurrently administered invented spelling task (a task in which phonemic awareness is absolutely essential) or with the Slosson Oral Reading Test ($r = .07$).

I want to add one more item to the "what's wrong" list, one alluded to in the current book—but one that concerns me so gravely that I want to use this opportunity to unpack it. This criticism focuses on what I take to be a sort of psychometric alchemy, and it turns on the metrics that DIBELS uses to scale student performance—rates (the number of X per minute) rather than accuracy (percentage of this domain the student exhibits control over). Scott Paris, in a hard-hitting critique of the ways in which lots of these tests of specific skills are used (2005), makes an important distinction between what he calls constrained and unconstrained skills. This distinction parallels one that I borrowed from the late James Squire, between mastery skills and growth constructs. Paris's constrained skills (my mastery skills) are phenomena—such as letter names, letter sounds, phonemic awareness, mechanics in writing—that we teach with the expectation that once kids demonstrate mastery, we can get on with something else. Paris's unconstrained skills (my growth constructs) are phenomena—such as composition, comprehension, word meaning, or critical thinking—that, by their very nature, cannot be mastered; they always exhibit capacity for even greater growth. We teach them not with the expectation that they get learned to mastery so we can go on to something more important, but with the expectation that they are the real stuff of literacy—the important things we go on to!

If one looks at DIBELS, it is clear that all of the tests, except the Oral Reading Fluency/Retell component, measure constrained (mastery) skills—things that are learned along the way to real reading. If the creators of DIBELS had chosen to report these phenomena on an accuracy scale rather than a rate scale, what they would have found is that for many of the skills, most

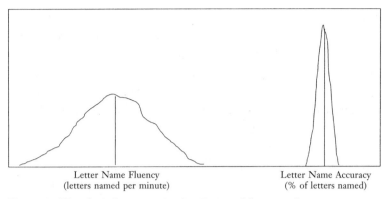

Letter Name Fluency
(letters named per minute)

Letter Name Accuracy
(% of letters named)

Figure 1: *Hypothetical comparative distribution of fluency and accuracy scores on letter naming*

students would reach a performance ceiling in either first or second grade. Such a distribution of scores is depicted in the right-hand side of Figure 1. But that same set of students who vary little in terms of the alphabet knowledge will vary considerably in their letter naming fluency (letters named per minute), as depicted in the left-hand side of Figure 1.

There is no magic, no alchemy, here. It is a direct application of a general rule about human performance: human beings alike in their capacity to perform a given task with accuracy and integrity will vary dramatically in the speed or fluency with which they perform it. This is true not only in reading but also in a range of cognitive and psychomotor tasks. It is part of our "human nature," if you will. It is also the case, again in a wide range of human performances, that speed or fluency correlates with general cognitive and psychomotor ability. The creators of DIBELS benefit from these two general laws. It permits them to show that performance on a highly constrained skill on which students perform at near mastery levels predicts scores on a more general unconstrained phenomenon (such as a standardized reading test score) if the accuracy index on that constrained skill is transformed into a fluency index. Why? For a lot of reasons, but directly to the point here is a long-standing rule of thumb in testing: other things being equal, the greater the variance on a test, the greater its reliability and, hence, the greater its capacity to demonstrate correlations with other measures of cognitive ability. This is what I was referring to earlier when I used the metaphor of psychometric alchemy. DIBELS, and any other test battery that uses rate rather than accuracy as an index of performance for a constrained skill, can demonstrate the concurrent or predictive validity of that measure to a greater degree than can a test battery that relies on accuracy.

The important question for a teacher or a school faculty is the "so what" question: What will you do differently instructionally if you know that Tommy names his letters or his phonemes at a slower rate than does Susana? Will we have Tommy practice naming letters faster? The same could be asked of the ubiquitous reading fluency measures we see all over America. What will we do with students who read accurately but slowly—have them engage in timed trials five days a week? Now we are back to the means-ends confusion discussed earlier—the problem that arises when an indicator of progress is elevated to the status of a curricular goal. I surely want kids to make progress on fluency—to read faster and with greater expression—as they mature (by the way, I also want them to know when to slow down—either to savor the language of an author or to puzzle over an enigmatic expression) as Flurkey demonstrates in his chapter. But I want them to make that progress on fluency because we provided them with a rich curriculum that ensured balanced development of a range of skills and a broad exposure to important ideas—not because we had them practice timed trials five times per week.

Changing My Mind

What would it take to convince me to change my mind about DIBELS? I like to think of myself, ultimately, as the quintessential empiricist—as a person who would be convinced by evidence that my a priori conceptual stand was misguided or just plain wrong. I also like to think of myself as an individual who has changed his mind often—whenever compelling evidence and logic forced me to reconsider my position and/or world view. To those unhappy, even outraged, by my critique, I do have an experiment in mind for DIBELS proponents and the folks in Reading First and No Child Left Behind who have, either directly or indirectly, promoted its use. It would require the DIBELS folks to move beyond criterion-related validity to validity related to the consequences of test use (Messick, 1989) to demonstrate that when DIBELS is used in the ways that its proponents suggest, good things happen to and for students, teachers, and parents. Messick coined the term *consequential validity* to capture the notion that the validity of tests is less about their internal character than about the decisions that are made when they are used to shape action in the real world. So here is my challenge to the DIBELS folks: Show me that when DIBELS is used to monitor and shape instruction (as it clearly is in the current milieu) it actually promotes growth on more significant and more global indicators of reading (and writing) development than are measured by DIBELS itself. If, as a result of using DIBELS to guide instruction, kids read more, read more *enthusiastically* and with *greater comprehension*, wrote with greater *facility*, and *felt better* about themselves as readers, then I would back off this critique and say, "You're right. Using DIBELS does help develop more avid, active, and efficacious readers and writers than other assessment tools."

In my experiment, there would be two large groups (with lots of relevant sub-populations): one using DIBELS and one using more global indicators to monitor progress and shape instruction. The two progress-monitoring assessments would be given at key points along the way, probably three times a year over a three- or four-year period (I'd propose grades K–3). At pre-specified intervals, we'd also administer more global, more growth-oriented assessments of reading and writing, at a minimum at the beginning of the study and at the end of each academic year. The key question would be whether teaching in a way to directly influence growth on DIBELS promoted incidental growth on the global measures to a greater degree than did teaching for growth with some alternative monitoring system. In other words, it would answer the question of whether DIBELS bore more positive consequences for kids than did some alternative. And if it did, I'd back off the critique I have offered—because the data would have demonstrated that the path to literacy is paved with letters, phonemes, and fluency, not, as I currently believe, with richer knowledge, more refined word meanings, and an extensive tool kit of useful strategies to make sense of text when the going gets tough. In this regard, I would note that Seay (this volume) does provide a "partial" answer to this question, albeit at a very broad level of analysis. She examined the changes in scores of Alabama students on NAEP reading and on the state's standardized reading test (SAT-10) as a function of either 2 or 3 years of participation in a Reading First program in which DIBELS was used to monitor and guide instruction. She notes little improvement on either of these external indicators as a function of Alabama's participation in Reading First (but it must be admitted that she did not disaggregate state assessment performance as a function of whether schools did or did not participate in Reading First). Even so, the anticipated gains in overall achievement have not been realized.

Coping in the Meantime

Finally, there is the question of what we do while we are waiting for this "millennium" study to be done. How do we cope with the reality of DIBELS? Here is where this book will be useful, for it outlines strong critiques that concerned educators and citizens can take to school boards and legislatures and suggests alternative models of responsible assessment—what could, and perhaps should, we be using to monitor student progress.

If I were working in a district or school where DIBELS was mandated, I'd insist that we develop and implement a set of parallel assessments that measure reading and writing in their more global, not their more atomistic, aspect—maybe something like running records with comprehension and response to literature, regular writing samples, and some index of spelling progress. And if kids were making progress on DIBELS but not the more global measures, I'd want to argue for a different sort of intervention than is typically promoted by DIBELS. And if kids were making progress on the more global measures but not DIBELS,

I'd want to know the sorts of compensatory mechanisms they were using in the absence of well-developed alphabetics.

The final thing I would do is to promote, at every opportunity, greater sensitivity to what I consider the two most important principles of good assessment policy. Principle #1 addresses the issue of how assessment relates to curriculum and suggests that we beware of putting the cart before the horse. The point is that assessments should reflect, not lead, curriculum and instruction. We need instructionally sensitive assessments, not assessment-sensitive curriculum.

> Principle #1: Never send a test out to do a curriculum's job!

The second principle relates to the question of consequences very directly. It admits that, other things being equal, people will teach to tests—even if in their heart of hearts they know they should not. Further, it suggests that the higher the stakes (consequences), the greater the likelihood that people will teach to a test. Hence, when stakes are high, so must be the level of challenge and the transparent authenticity of the test.

> Principle #2: The higher the stakes, the greater must be the challenge and the authenticity of the assessment.

The worst situation imaginable is high stakes and low challenge—for that combination will drive instruction to the lowest common denominator and guarantee that our lowest achieving students will never get to the "good stuff" in our curriculum because they will spend all of their time working on the "basics."

Now to the Book

As I said at the outset, I agreed to write this foreword because I think the crisis of curriculum promoted by excessive reliance on componential measures of reading such as DIBELS is serious—palpable, you can feel it and almost touch it—in our schools when you view the consequences and hear the stories of parents and teachers and students whose lives are directly influenced by these assessments—and by DIBELS in particular. The book is important to those who wish to resist this sort of curricular mandate because it offers strong arguments and evidence to support that effort. It is my hope that the book will also spur reading and measurement researchers to pursue rigorous research to address some of the unanswered questions that remain before us regarding the conceptual, psychometric, and pragmatic aspects of assessment policy. In fact, I would hope that the federal Department of Education would seize the opportunity to ensure that the assessments it promotes are held to the gold standard of assessment scholarship and fund studies to evaluate the validity and impact of various sorts of assessment tools, including DIBELS.

Happy reading on the road to action in the policy arena—at every level: local, state, and national.

References

Good, R. H., & Jefferson, G. 1998. *Contemporary Perspectives on Curriculum-based Measurement Validity*. New York: The Guilford Press.

Good, R. H., Kaminski, R. A. 2002. *DIBELS Oral Reading Fluency Passages for First Through Third Grades* (Technical Report No. 10). Eugene, OR: University of Oregon.

Manzo, K. 2005. "National Clout of DIBELS Test Draws Scrutiny." *Education Week* 25 (5): 1, 12.

Manzo, K. 2005. "States Pressed to Refashion Reading First Grant Designs." *Education Week* 25 (2): 1, 24–25.

Messick, S. 1989. "Validity." In *Educational Measurement*, 3rd ed., edited by R. L. Linn. New York: Macmillan.

National Institute of Child Health and Human Development. Report of the National Reading Panel. 2000. *Teaching Children to Read: An Evidence-based Assessment of the Scientific Research Literature on Reading and Its Implications for Reading Instruction* (NIH Publication No. 00-4769). Washington, DC: U.S. Government Printing Office.

Paris, S. G. 2005. "Reinterpreting the development of reading skills." *Reading Research Quarterly* 40 (2): 184–202.

Pearson, P. D. 2001. "Life in the radical middle: A personal apology for a balanced view of reading." In *Reading Researchers in Search of Common Ground,* edited by R. Flippo. Newark, DE: International Reading Association.

Pressley, M., Hilden, K., & Shankland, R. 2005. *An Evaluation of End-Grade-3 Dynamic Indicators of Basic Early Literacy Skills (DIBELS): Speed Reading Without Comprehension, Predicting Little.* East Lansing, MI: Literacy Achievement Research Center, technical report.

Tindall, G., Marston, D., & Deno, S. L. 1983. *The Reliability of Direct and Repeated Measurement* (Research Rep. No. 109). Minneapolis: University of Minnesota Institute for Research on Learning Disabilities.

Prologue
DIBELS: One Family's Journey

I can think of no better prologue to this critique of
DIBELS than this diary of one family's experience with DIBELS.
KSG

Note 1: Mid-September, 2005

I've been crying for the better part of two days because my family has encountered the horror of DIBELS. My husband and I
just moved from Portland, Oregon—where our son, Ellis, had a
wonderful kindergarten experience—to a rural town in the north-
eastern section of the state.

Ellis is starting first grade at Joseph Elementary. We were surprised but not alarmed to learn from the first grade teacher that
all incoming first graders (according to her) knew how to read.
Ellis does not know how to read, nor do we support a teaching
philosophy that would make reading mandatory for entering or
even finishing first grade.

After teaching Ellis for thirteen days, the first-grade teacher
at Joseph Elementary asked us for an immediate conference to
discuss his progress. She gave us two choices: Ellis could repeat
kindergarten or could be held back at the end of first grade. These
options were presented to us as the best solution for Ellis to keep
him from being "stigmatized because he was below the benchmark in two specific DIBELS scores, phoneme recognition and
nonsense words. (Ellis was average to above-average for his class
in the other DIBELS areas. She did not address the issue of other
subjects such as math and science where we are confident he'd

be ahead of his class since his Portland school had a math and science focused curriculum and we look over his daily school work when he arrives home.

The main issue for us is Joseph Elementary's overreliance on standardized testing and teaching methods solely designed to support test success—the child's well-being be damned. Another issue is the lack of respect and support for students who move across state and change schools. Whatever happened to extra support, such as tutors or make-up lessons conducted at home? The school staff did not offer these solutions; additionally, we received teaching materials only after we requested them.

Unfortunately, the only other public school nearby also uses DIBELS. We are currently debating the option of homeschooling and supplementing our son's education to make up for what is left out of the public school curriculum in order to focus so heavily on standardized tests. This trade-off has led to a disappearance of creativity, diversity, philosophical inquiry, and fun in our public schools; it seems so monumental and ingrained in the current system that we are sickened at the thought of keeping Ellis in such an environment. We will not be holding back our bright, confident, tender-hearted, funny, and delightful son.

Note 2:

One of my favorite music groups is the Violent Femmes (I experienced high school in the early 80s). The song that used to make us all scream at the top of our lungs was "Kiss Off"; it came back to me today in all its brilliance for one particular line:

> I HOPE YOU KNOW THIS WILL GO DOWN ON YOUR
> PERMANENT RECORD.

At Joseph Elementary (grades K–4) the students are tested approximately once a month by the Title I coordinator. These scores are then transmitted to the University of Oregon.

Ellis' first test had the following scores; the numbers in parentheses represent the range of the fifteen other students in his class:

Letter Naming Fluency: 28 (11–45)

Phoneme Segmentation Fluency: 4 (4–68)

Word Use Fluency: 41 (14–63)

Nonsense Word Fluency: 6 (6–44)

No one at Joseph Elementary ever discussed DIBELS and the monthly testing when we enrolled Ellis. No one has ever discussed the transmission of his test scores either. Welcome to *1984*.

About the nonsense word portion of DIBELS: Ellis is a very thoughtful and cautious boy, so careful and deliberative is exactly how he would approach a test. He is not one to be rushed, whether it's getting his shoes on or painting a picture.

I would like to report that the first-grade teacher is young and inexperienced, but, in fact, she is neither—my guess would be she's been teaching at least twenty-five years. She also seems to truly believe in DIBELS, which is more horrifying than those who are trapped by it and NCLB.

I spent time in Ellis' classroom yesterday; Bob and I will be going next week as well. What I saw makes me unable to give my son to such a rigid and unimaginative place. There was nothing redeeming about his day. Not even art was fun.

I've met with people homeschooling their children nearby. At this point, that is our plan.

Note 3: Oct. 26, 2005

September 14th, the day we met with Ellis' teacher to discuss his progress, was the beginning of a whirlwind education on DIBELS. That evening, I spent about five hours reading everything I could find. I plan to continue to fight whether or not my son is in school. But Ellis' teacher wholeheartedly believes in DIBELS and teaches to the test for forty-five minutes, twice a day.

During Ellis' first two weeks at Joseph Elementary, he was pulled out for extra instruction every day. He was an absolute mess—tired, cranky, short-tempered—and he was becoming depressed.

On Monday, October 7, Ellis came to the decision on his own to not go to school any more. That day, he seemed especially tired and depressed. Bob and I had already decided that sending him back to school was detrimental to all of us. We had wrestled with how to tell Ellis he wasn't going back to school; for days we just said we wanted him to take time off. And then on Wednesday, he was having one meltdown after another, so I took him aside at a quiet area in the park. Ever since he'd been going to Joseph Elementary he seemed tired, grumpy, and not quite himself, and I asked him what he thought we could do to help him. He said, "Stop sending me to school." We can sure support that wish!

When we then met with the principal to discuss why we were withdrawing Ellis, she gave us the Benchmark Assessment used to test him. We found out that he was tested first on August 26th and again September 28th. It was infuriating to know that even with the improvement shown in that short period of time, Ellis' teacher wanted him to repeat kindergarten. It was clear to us that DIBELS is double punishment: DIBELS, in and of itself, and the expectation that kindergartners must enter first grade with a specific and narrow range of reading skills in spite of their other skills and knowledge.

Getting an inside look at the test was additional proof of how lousy DIBELS is. For example, the font used in the letter naming fluency section was one where the lower case *g* and *a* look alike, which is neither the way children are taught to write them nor the font used in children's books. Also, the letter *l* looks just like the number one, further confusing students. Ellis' test twice indicated that he called the *l* a *1*—or was it the *1* an *l*?

We have been homeschooling now for four weeks and Ellis' change back to his regular lovely self is astounding, although not surprising after witnessing his school day. We are not willing to sacrifice our child to that hellhole. I will, however, continue to do what I can to change what is happening to our public schools because of DIBELS.

A Critical Review of DIBELS

KEN GOODMAN, Professor Emeritus,
Language Reading and Culture
University of Arizona, Tucson

DIBELS Dynamic Indicators of Basic Early Literacy Skills, Sixth Edition
Edited by Roland Good and Ruth A. Kaminski
Published by IDEA (Institute for the Development of Educational
 Achievement)
Director: Dr. Edward J. Kame'enui (now Commissioner for Special
 Education Research and Director of the National Center for
 Special Education Research, U.S. Department of Education)
Note: The entire test including examiner's manuals and test and
scoring materials is downloadable, and this review is based on a critical
analysis of the most current edition provided on the Internet at
http://dibels.uoregon.edu/.

Why a Critical Review of DIBELS?

DIBELS is not just an early literacy test. In thousands of schools
all over the United States, children from kindergarten to third
grade (and in some schools beyond third grade) are taking the test
three or more times a semester. Teachers are required to group
learners and build instruction around the scores. Teachers are
evaluated on the DIBELS scores their pupils achieve. Reading text
publishers are tailoring their programs to use with DIBELS. And
academic and life decisions for children, starting in kindergarten,
including promotion and failure, are being made according to
DIBELS scores.

Note from a teacher

We're trying to keep it in a realistic place and not let it run our lives totally. . . . We're not using DIBELS because we want to use it or because it gives helpful information, because it doesn't, we're using it because Reading First requires it. We then have to do additional assessments to find out what kids really need. We feel like we're assessing constantly. Some schools are posting fluency scores of children in a classroom and then the students have race cars, in the form of bulletin boards, where they are trying to race to the speed goal. On the phoneme segmentation part, some kindergarten classrooms have been known to drill and practice the segmentation while kids are in lines waiting for the restroom.

According to the official DIBELS website, "for the 2004–2005 school year, 8293 schools used the DIBELS Data System across 2582 districts in 49 states and Canada, totaling over 1.7 million students (K–3)." The DIBELS Data System, a computerized system housed at the University of Oregon, analyses data submitted by schools and sends reports back on which pupils are progressing or not and how the teachers and schools should proceed. The state of New Mexico, among others, provides every teacher with a Palm Pilot computer that contains the DIBELS scoring system so the pupils' scores can be directly sent to the state and to Oregon for processing and quick response. Since the entire test is downloadable and since many states mandate use of DIBELS in their No Child Left Behind (NCLB) Reading First programs, it is likely that it is even more widely used.

Education Week states:

> DIBELS has become a catchphrase in the schoolhouse and the statehouse as officials look to test data to inform instruction, to identify children at risk of failure in reading, and to hold schools accountable for student achievement. (Manzo 2005)

Education Week also reports that state officials believe they were coerced by Washington officials administering NCLB to use DIBELS or risk not getting funded:

> The battery of tests was not the first choice for Illinois and some states applying for the federal money. In fact, a number of states had intended to use other assessments for screening children and gauging progress in Reading First schools. They changed their plans, they maintain, after federal officials and consultants pres-

sured them to include DIBELS in their grant proposal as a condition for approval." (Manzo 2005)

In this critique, I will:

1. Provide a concise summary of each subtest and consider the stated intentions of the authors of DIBELS for the whole test and for each of the subtests. (See Appendix for summaries.)

2. Examine the view of reading and reading development the DIBELS authors espouse and the extent to which the test and subtests are consistent with that view and how fully reading is tested by DIBELS according to their own view.

3. Examine each subtest to see how it is constructed and the extent to which it tests what it is intended to test. In particular, I will look at factors in the design and execution of the test items and administration of the test that might make it difficult for examiners to be consistent in administering the test or might result in pupil responses that could misrepresent abilities.

> **Note from a teacher**
>
> I have seen the horrors that have hit teachers in our district as a result of the DIBELS being mandated in our district at all grade levels, K–5. Not only is it mandated three times yearly, but teachers are expected to do the monitor portion of the test once each month, regardless of how the student is reading. In addition to that, any child who receives the label "Needs Extensive Intervention" as a result of the first testing must be monitored with a "fluency passage" every other week.
>
> No test of any kind for any purpose has ever had this kind of status across American schools. Because of the political process in which DIBELS has been mandated, it has rarely, if ever, been subject to the careful review required in legally mandated adoption procedures used in school districts and states in choosing assessments. It is time that this test be subjected to critical review.

4. Examine the possibilities that the test and subtests could misrepresent the success or failure of pupils in development within the testers' view of reading.

5. Critique the DIBELS view of reading and of reading development and consider what imposition of this view does to curriculum, teacher-pupil relations, and reading development, and how it can impact the lives of students and teachers.

The Stated Intentions of the Authors of DIBELS for the Whole Test and for Each of the Subtests

The DIBELS website states the following:

> The Dynamic Indicators of Basic Early Literacy Skills (DIBELS) are [sic] a set of standardized, individually administered measures of early literacy development. They are designed to be short (one minute) fluency measures used to regularly monitor the development of prereading and early reading skills.
>
> The measures were developed upon the essential early literacy domains discussed in both the National Reading Panel (2000) and National Research Council (1998) reports to assess student development of phonological awareness, alphabetic understanding, and automaticity and fluency with the code. Each measure has been thoroughly researched and demonstrated to be reliable and valid indicators of early literacy development and predictive of later reading proficiency to aid in the early identification of students who are not progressing as expected. When used as recommended, the results can be used to evaluate individual student development as well as provide grade-level feedback toward validated instructional objectives.

A note to readers of this critique

It's my hope that teachers, parents, and educational decision makers will all find this critique useful. I've tried to avoid jargon and unnecessary technical and linguistic terminology. For purposes of clarity that's not always been possible, particularly since those mandating DIBELS have claimed that it is based in science. Often the DIBELS authors use undefined technical terms which must be examined. Parents may want to consider, if they find issues involving the subtests and their contents difficult to understand, how the test must seem to five, six, seven, and eight year olds. And ultimately it is the way the test affects the children that is most important. I've included in sidebars insightful comments from teachers who see the effects of DIBELS in their classrooms.

The manual for administrating DIBELS says further that:

> The DIBELS is [sic] an assessment system designed to assess all students' progress (kindergarten through third grade) on the big ideas of early literacy development in a standardized, time efficient manner. We recommend assessing students at the beginning, middle, and end of an academic year to allow for timely instructional feedback.

The phrase *Big Ideas* is one used on the University of Oregon IDEA (Institute for the Development of Educational Achievement) website to correspond to the major "findings" of the National Reading Panel. IDEA is the parent organization of DIBELS and proceeds from DIBELS support its research and activities. Schools pay $1 for processing by DIBELS Data System (IDEA) for each test for each pupil. Since they report that last year 1.7 million pupils used this system, that would mean $5.1 million income for IDEA.

According to the IDEA website there are five Big Ideas in beginning reading:

1. Phonemic Awareness: The ability to hear and manipulate sounds in words.[1]
2. Alphabetic Principle: The ability to associate sounds with letters and use these sounds to form words.
3. Fluency with Text: The effortless, automatic ability to read words in connected text.
4. Vocabulary: The ability to understand (receptive) and use (expressive) words to acquire and convey meaning.
5. Comprehension: The complex cognitive process involving the intentional interaction between reader and text to convey meaning.

The IDEA website relates four of the DIBELS subtests to three of these Big Ideas:

Big Idea of Literacy	DIBELS Measure
Phonological Awareness	Initial Sounds Fluency
	Phoneme Segmentation Fluency
Alphabetic Principle	Nonsense Word Fluency
Fluency with Text	Oral Reading Fluency

Notice that Big Ideas 4, Vocabulary, and 5, Comprehension are separate Big Ideas which follow 3, Fluency with Text, and are not tested by DIBELS according to these tables. The authors

---

[1]In the IDEA and DIBELS websites, *phonemic awareness* and *phonological awareness* seem to be used interchangeably.

consider that the skills measured by the subtests are sequential stepping stones in reading development: "As stepping stones to literacy development, it means that performance on one of the DIBELS measures is predictive of performance on the next appropriate DIBELS measure(s)." In practice this means that children who fail to reach the benchmark for a given subtest are not ready to go on and must receive intensive practice and pass the subtest before going on.

And in fact the authors of DIBELS provide a sequence for administrating the tests from kindergarten through third grade. Three subtests are used sequentially in kindergarten, representing Big Ideas 1, "Phonemic Awareness: The ability to hear and manipulate sounds in words" and 2, "Alphabetic Principle: The ability to associate sounds with letters and use these sounds to form words." The three tests are Initial Sounds Fluency, Phoneme Segmentation Fluency, and Nonsense Word Fluency. Although it doesn't appear in the chart, the manual for kindergarten administration shows Word Use Fluency as optional. Also optional is Letter Naming Fluency (LNF). See Figure 1.

In first grade, the last two of those tests are continued representing the first two Big Ideas, and another test, Oral Reading Fluency, is added in mid-first grade for Big Idea 3, "Fluency with Text: The effortless, automatic ability to read words in connected text." Letter Naming Fluency is also provided but not claimed to relate to a Big Idea. Still, its appearance as first in the sequence of the subtests in the manual suggests the authors also consider it a stepping stone. Two optional tests are offered, Retelling Fluency (to be administered with Oral Reading Fluency) and Word Use Fluency. These appear to relate to Big Ideas 4 and 5, though they are not shown in these charts for K–3 use of DIBELS. See Figure 2.

In grades two and three only the last test is continued. Though this chart doesn't show it, at the beginning of second grade Nonsense Word Fluency is also administered. Retelling Fluency (to be administered with Oral Reading Fluency) and Word Use Fluency are, according to the manual, optional in both second and third grades. See Figure 3.

Big Idea Assessed	Beginning-of-Year	Mid-Year	End-of-Year
Phonological Awareness	Initial Sounds Fluency (ISF)	Initial Sounds Fluency (ISF)	
Phonological Awareness		Phoneme Segmentation Fluency (PSF)	Phoneme Segmentation Fluency (PSF)
Alphabetic Principle		Nonsense Word Fluency (NWF)	Nonsense Word Fluency (NWF)

Figure 1 *Kindergarten DIBELS Assessment Schedule*

Big Idea Assessed	Beginning-of-Year	Mid-Year	End-of-Year
Phonological Awareness	Phoneme Segmentation Fluency (PSF)	Phoneme Segmentation Fluency (PSF)	Phoneme Segmentation Fluency (PSF)
Alphabetic Principle	Nonsense Word Fluency (NWF)	Nonsense Word Fluency (NWF)	Nonsense Word Fluency (NWF)
Fluency with Connected Text		Oral Reading Fluency (ORF)	Oral Reading Fluency (ORF)

Figure 2 *First Grade DIBELS Assessment Schedule*

Big Idea Assessed	Beginning-of-Year	Mid-Year	End-of-Year
Fluency with Connected Text	Oral Reading Fluency (ORF)	Oral Reading Fluency (ORF)	Oral Reading Fluency (ORF)

Figure 3 *Second and Third Grade DIBELS Assessment Schedule*

Administering and Scoring the DIBELS Measures

The DIBELS manual provides explicit detailed procedures for administering the subtests and requires strict adherence to them:

> Each DIBELS measure has standardized administration and scoring procedures so that the scores have meaning. Deviating from or modifying the administration or scoring procedures of any of the measures decreases or minimizes the validity of the score's meaning. Most educational personnel can be trained to reliably and accurately administer these measures with the materials available on the DIBELS website.

> **A note to the reader**
>
> A brief review of each subtest and its stated purpose in relation to the Big Ideas can be found in the Appendix. Readers unfamiliar with DIBELS may want to read that before proceeding.

Collecting student performance data on all students sounds intimidating at first. However, because testing takes less than ten minutes per child, it can be accomplished in each school with a little planning.

Contained in the above are two key assumptions the DIBELS authors make:

1. That suitably "trained" testers will administer and score the tests in a uniform way.
2. That a few minutes of performance on a set of reduced discrete tasks can usefully and fairly represent progress in reading development.

Though testing each child may only take ten minutes, testing a classroom of twenty-five children would take 250 minutes of teacher time or the time of someone other than the teacher to administer the test. Multiply that by the required three tests a year—plus progress testing as frequently as weekly—and the testing time becomes a major intrusion on instructional time.

A Note on Fluency

Each DIBELS subtest has a name including the word *fluency*. Though the authors do not say so in the manuals, fluency is used here to mean speed and accuracy in the performance of a tested task. Just as there is the assumption that each subtest is a sequential stepping stone toward becoming a reader, there is also the assumption that being fast and accurate—in naming letters for example—leads to becoming fast and accurate at identifying initial sounds and subsequently becoming a fluent reader, defined by the DIBELS authors as being an accurate and fast reader.

Summary of The DIBELS Authors' View of Reading and Reading Development

DIBELS is committed to testing the Big Ideas as IDEA, its parent, has stated them and as derived from the National Reading Panel report. But its focus is on the first three: *phonological awareness*, *alphabetic principle*, and *fluency with connected text*. The word *fluency* is used in each subtest name and by it the authors show their belief that development in reading and all its component skills involve achieving speed and accuracy. DIBELS also includes a test of letter naming, although the authors indicate that it does not relate to the Big IDEAS and does not predict success in reading. They also have added to their test of fluency with connected text an optional Retelling Fluency score to offer a measure of comprehension, though they make clear the former is a sufficient test of reading competence and comprehension. A test of Word Use Fluency (WUF) is also provided apparently to correspond to Big Idea 4, Vocabulary. Though it is also optional, WUF is the one subtest to be used from kindergarten through third grade.

The DIBELS View of Reading

Though the authors do not state in the manual the definition of reading they operate from, the tests reveal that they believe that competent reading is the ability to read words rapidly and accurately and that comprehension is the result of such rapid, accurate reading. The authors also believe that what happens in one minute of reading happens in all of reading. It's likely that they do not explicitly state their definition of reading because they don't see any need to define reading since they have not considered that there could be any other definitions.

The DIBELS View of Reading Development

Implicit in the choices the authors make of what to test in each subtest, how the tests are sequenced, and how each component is tested is a view of reading development that involves a single universal sequence of mastering component skills. In their view, each skill as tested is a necessary prerequisite to each other and to competent reading.

When Does Reading Instruction Begin?

It is important to note that the authors of DIBELS assume that formal reading instruction should begin in kindergarten. In fact, it recommends using one subtest, Initial Sound Fluency (ISF), in preschool. This is no small matter, because where DIBELS is in use it plays a major role in the kindergarten curriculum and success or failure in kindergarten will be judged in terms of DIBELS. Parents need to understand that this is a historical change in the role and function of kindergarten as conceived by its nineteenth-century pioneers as a place for play and socialization into school. The name says it: a garden for children. And there is a long history of controversy over whether reading instruction should be part of the kindergarten curriculum. Early childhood educators ask whether a particular activity is "developmentally appropriate." Simply, is it suitable for very young children? Should five year olds be repeatedly tested with timed tests? Should those who can't perform on these one-minute tests be drilled on naming letters and sounding out words while their classmates play? And should children come to see themselves as failures before they even start first grade?

While the majority of American children attend kindergarten, kindergarten is not universal in the United States. In a number of states attendance in kindergarten is not mandatory and in some states local districts are not required to offer kindergarten. A recent survey reports:

> Most states do not require children to attend kindergarten, and eight states (Alaska, Colorado, Idaho, New Hampshire, New Jersey, New York, North Dakota, Pennsylvania) do not require

school districts to offer kindergarten. Only fourteen states require age-eligible children to attend at least a half day of kindergarten. Similarly, only nine states (Alabama, Arkansas, Georgia, Louisiana, Maryland, Mississippi, North Carolina, South Carolina, West Virginia) require school districts to offer full-day kindergarten, and two states (Louisiana and West Virginia) require that children attend full-day programs. (Kauerz 2005)

By pressuring states to require use of DIBELS in kindergarten, the federal government is in effect mandating kindergarten, taking away parental choice, and depriving children of a small but important part of childhood.

Reductionism

Because DIBELS is designed to be "quick and easy," each component skill is reduced to a task that can be tested in a minute. So, in fact, only a reduced aspect of each Big Idea is actually tested. The following list compares what each test reduces the claimed component skills to in contrast to what it says it is intended to measure:

Letter Naming Fluency (LNF) is intended to measure letter knowledge.	LNF actually tests the ability to name upper- and lowercase letters presented in a single font rapidly and accurately.
Initial Sounds Fluency (ISF) and Phoneme Segmentation Fluency (PSF) are intended to test phonological (also called phonemic) awareness.	ISF actually tests the ability to identify initial sounds of words that name pictures rapidly and accurately.
	PSF actually tests the ability to abstract the component sounds (sound out) from single syllable words accurately and fluently.

Nonsense Word Fluency (NWF) is intended to measure control of the "alphabetic principle."

NWF actually tests the ability of children to match letters to sounds either one at a time or by "saying" a whole nonsense syllable accurately and rapidly.

Oral Reading Fluency (ORF) is intended to test the ability to read and make sense of connected text.

ORF actually tests the ability to read words in a short, usually first-person, passage rapidly and accurately.

Retelling Fluency (RF) is intended to provide further evidence of comprehension of the passages read in ORF.

RF actually tests the ability to rapidly produce a number of words that retell the passage read and stay on track.

Word Use Fluency (WUF) is intended to measure vocabulary defined in DIBELS as the ability to define and/or use words. (Actually, vocabulary has two aspects: *productive* vocabulary is the ability to use words effectively and *receptive* vocabulary is the ability to understand the words one hears or reads.)

WUF does not test receptive vocabulary, which is certainly more involved in reading than productive vocabulary. WUF actually tests the ability to rapidly produce a number of words that "use" a word in an utterance that defines or represents an acceptable use of a word. A peculiarity of this test is that the score is the number of words in each responsive utterance rather than a judgment of the quality of the use. In a test that values accuracy, accurate word use is not measured in the WUF.

In summary, DIBELS is based on a view of reading development as involving a mastery of a sequenced set of skills, but each component skill is reduced to an aspect that can be tested in one minute.

Reification

The DIBELS authors are guilty of another major assessment error: reification. Simply, this means that by letting a one-minute reduced task represent a larger concept, they reify the test they've created. That is, they treat it as if it really is what the name suggests it is. So a test that counts the number of right words produced in one minute in reading a passage is treated as if it actually measures oral reading fluency. In this case, the authors make a bold claim on their website: "In general, oral reading fluency provides one of the best measures of reading competence, including comprehension, for children in first through third grades." Here they equate a score that represents correct words read in one minute with the totality of reading competently with comprehension—an ultimate *reification*.

> **Note from a DIBEL trainee**
>
> At one point in the training, the presenter was troubleshooting with teachers about how to respond to a student whose voice was inaudible. The presenter reminded teachers that they could stop the test and give a different version of it to the student on another day. She also stated that teachers could mark test items wrong if they weren't sure of what they heard the student say because it's better to identify a student for help than to miss a student who might need intervention. She continued by saying that students who have been incorrectly identified will exit the intervention program quickly and no harm will have been done.

Timed Tests

As indicated above, every subtest of DIBELS is timed and a great deal is made of what a child can do in one minute. While it is true that most other tests are timed, there is some evidence that the use of timed tests disadvantages some learners and advantages others. Those who are more cautious, more perfectionist, more thoughtful, more curious, more talkative, or just slow are likely to suffer in a timed test. Those who are eager, frenetic, impetuous, or drilled for the tests are likely to be advantaged.

Young children in the process of becoming literate, faced with one-minute tests, may be grossly misrepresented by their scores. Children who already are coming to understand that reading is supposed to make sense are likely to be underscored. That is a particular problem with Nonsense Word Fluency (NWF), since children who try to find sense in nonsense may be counted wrong or lose time because of comments they make on the items. But in general the more thoughtful and concerned with the meaning a young reader is the more likely they are to perform more slowly or to lose time as they are distracted by a search for meaning.

Learning To Be Fast

The DIBELS authors themselves admit children, and even teachers, may learn a "misrule" that doing each task as fast as possible is more important than anything else in scoring well on DIBELS. In fact that is not a misrule in this test. *It is the rule.* With so much at stake for both pupils and teachers, not to mention administrators, it's unavoidable that practice for DIBELS will emphasize speed. And speed is teachable so that progress from one testing to another may result from children being drilled on doing each test as fast as possible. What appears to be progress in reading development is more likely to be evidence of faster performance on the test.

> **Note from a teacher**
>
> Some students have realized in taking the DIBELS that it doesn't matter how you read, just read it fast. These students have learned to skip the big words and just say the high frequency words in the passage as fast as they can. Many of these students received the higher scores in the testing, yet are the poorest readers.

Understanding the Tasks

Young children often can be made to look less proficient than they are if they do not understand the tasks they are being asked to perform. This is particularly aggravated in DIBELS by the restrictions on the testers to stay with the exact wording of the instructions and specific constraints on the prompts they may offer. For example, one child in response to the Letter Naming

Fluency subtest responded to each letter with a child's name. The only prompt the tester is permitted is "remember names, not sounds," which doesn't solve this child's problem. There must be many five and six year olds who don't know that letters have names but still know the names of letters. Researchers with young children have been aware that they may need to be very careful of the language they use in eliciting responses from children.

In each of the subtests, but in some more than others, the tester has a difficult job watching a stopwatch and making a series of judgments while marking pupil responses as correct or incorrect all in one minute. Teachers report the stopwatch is also distracting to the children. The performance is not tape recorded so there is no way for the tester to confirm or disconfirm what was heard. This is more difficult if children speak softly, put their hands over their mouths, speak an unfamiliar dialect, or have missing front teeth, all common characteristics of 5–8 year olds. So it is highly unlikely the scoring can be uniform or accurate on one-minute tests.

Note from a teacher

Kids are tested in our district by a team of testers who take kids one at a time and do the test. These people are strangers to the kindergarten child, and the students have never seen them or the room prior to the testing. One of my students came back and said he had been very good. "You will be proud of me! I didn't talk to strangers!" His scores were each a zero!

Dialect, Second Language, and Immature Speech

To their credit, the authors tell testers they may count dialect or articulation variants as correct and to use "professional judgment" in doing so. But they offer no special training in achieving this goal and the score sheet for evaluating testers does not include such judgments. My own experience in doing miscue analysis with both teachers and research assistants with considerable linguistic education is that making judgments about unfamiliar dialects is not easy and requires great sensitivity. It is most likely that many minority and immigrant children will be scored low for this reason, particularly since the manual provides just a single chart for judging acceptability of responses. Another aspect which the authors do not seem to have considered is that the testers also speak a dialect of English which may or not be equally familiar to all of their pupils. So the children may not hear what the tester thinks they are hearing. In my dialect, *Mary*, *merry*, and *marry* sound the same. But a teacher from another dialect community might say them all differently.

Benevolence and Professional Judgment   For these and other reasons it is very likely that biases will affect the scoring of the subtests. Is the tester being strict and attempting to let the chips fall where they may and thus likely to score responses as incorrect? Or is the tester sympathetic with the children and giving them the benefit of the doubt? Is the tester inconsistent, unconsciously letting overall judgments of the children influence scoring? In most cases the children are being tested by someone other than their teacher. While the intention may be to avoid bias in favor of the learner, many young children will perform less well when the tester is a stranger.

Teaching to the Test

There is an assumption built into DIBELS that improvement in performance over time on a given subtest is evidence of progress in becoming a reader. And teachers are told to provide intensive instruction for low-scoring children. With each test so specific in what it tests it should not be surprising that teachers tend to explicitly teach the test task. How else could they help children improve their scores? And it's only a small step beyond that, with the entire test available online, that some teachers go the next step and actually rehearse their pupils on the test. A parent could also download the test and practice it with the child at home. For that matter there are plenty of computer-savvy primary grade kids who could go

> **Note from a teacher**
>
> I have interjected at every meeting that we are not looking at the children but at a meaningless timed fluency for only a minute. I have been told basically to be quiet because this is what the district wants. I am an experienced teacher of reading and realized what this was doing to my children.
>
> After trying to talk to other teachers in my building, initiate professional learning communities where teachers read and talk together, and so on. I have resorted to altering my fluency scores. No, I do not want to do this, but my dishonesty is to protect my students from this paranoia that has taken over our schools.

From the DIBELS manual

Message to Parents: You should not use these materials to coach your child. If your child is being tested by his or her school, coaching them on the materials will invalidate the results. DIBELS is never used to grade your child; instead, it is used to identify students who need additional instructional support. If you coach your child, you may be removing instructional support that he or she needs.

online to get the test. Does any of this actually happen? With the stakes this high for DIBELS, I have no doubt.

Quantitative versus Qualitative Judgments

The DIBELS authors believe that a quantitative right/wrong score can measure any aspect of reading, including comprehension. It is the number of correct words in a passage that are read correctly in a minute and not what else is going on in the reading that is scored. Even in retelling, it is the number of words used in the retelling that is the score and not how complete the retelling is or whether it reflects theme, plot, characterization, etc. So over and over in each task it is how much is accurately completed in a minute and not the quality of the performance that is valued. Partly this is the result of the use of one-minute tests. There simply is not enough data for qualitative judgments; but it is also because the authors believe that right/wrong scores are sufficient to know whether young readers are moving toward making sense of their reading.

Parts and Wholes

Clearly DIBELS is based on the view that, in reading, the whole is the sum of the parts. So learning to read is learning letter names, identifying initial sounds, sounding out words, breaking nonsense into component sounds, etc. Even on the task of reading connected texts, reading is treated as accurately saying the names of words. That creates a fragmented view of progress in reading but it also leads to instruction that focuses on

Note from a teacher

Kindergarten kids like to talk. When given a page of letters to identify, they like to say "K, that's for Katie. Dd is for my dad and it's his birthday today and we got him a new shirt." Those kinds of responses do not get the required number of letters identified per minute. They are wonderful associations that give letters meaning. They cause a child to be listed as needing intensive intervention.

reduced aspects rather than on opportunities to make sense of meaningful texts.

How Well Does Each Subtest Succeed in Measuring What It Purports to Measure?

A close examination of each subtest reveals a number of problems that jeopardize the value of the scores pupils achieve and the judgments based on these scores. In this section I'll closely examine each subtest.

Problems with Letter Naming Fluency (LNF)

I've already mentioned the issue of young children not understanding that letters have names. As in other subtests there is a three-second rule. If a child does not name a letter, the tester says the name and points to the next letter and says, "What letter?" There is throughout DIBELS a kind of minimalism: short one-minute tests, short instructions, short minimal prompts, short pauses for correct answers. So the timid or thoughtful child is penalized. Furthermore, it is unstated and unclear why the child is told the name of the letter after three seconds. Perhaps the authors think the child will learn for the next testing by hearing the name. Children may infer, however, that if they have doubt they should wait for the tester and not try.

It's unclear in any case why LNF should be a timed test at all. If the goal is to find out whether a child knows the names of the letters, there are three possibilities: The child knows them all, the child knows some but not others, or the child knows none. What does it matter how long it takes a given child to show that? And how will practicing saying letter names faster to improve subsequent test performance benefit a child in becoming a reader? This is a question that needs to be asked with every DIBELS subtest: How will practice to improve the score on the test contribute to the child becoming an effective and efficient reader?

There is another problem with the scoring of this test and others. There is a difference between a child who slowly but correctly identifies every letter attempted and the child who rushes along and gets a third of the letters wrong. But the score is the number right in either case. This test is discontinued at the third kindergarten testing, which implies the authors' view that all kindergarten pupils should know all letter names by the end of kindergarten. And what of those children who don't know all the letter names? Will they repeat kindergarten?

Problems with Initial Sound Fluency (ISF)

Initial Sound Fluency (ISF) is the only subtest that is indicated to begin in preschool though the authors of the manual do not provide a reason. Preschool teachers, particularly those such as Head Start teachers who are on school campuses, report that they are being pressured to get their pupils ready for DIBELS testing in kindergarten. Logically then, should parents use it to get their kids ready for preschool?

In this subtest, whether the child understands the task or not is important. Consider the task: The child is shown a page with four unrelated pictures. The tester says, "This is . . ." and uses a single word, usually a noun, to name each of four pictures, i.e., "*tomato, cub, plate, doughnut,*" pointing to each picture as it is named. Then the tester says, "Which picture begins with /d/?" (the sound, not the letter name). In each set, the fourth question is different— "What sound does *plate* start with?"

Note from a teacher

Cute little ELL kids just stare up at you, especially the kindergarten students. The pictures in DIBELS are so ridiculous—for example, this is a *cub*, and the ELL students said, "no, that's a bear," and the teacher had to say, "no it's a cub." You're not supposed to say anything else, so the teacher didn't feel she could say that's a baby bear. So when the teacher said, "point to the picture that says *c*," the ELL kindergartners just randomly point. It's not that they don't know the sound, but that they don't know what the picture is.

To be successful, the child must remember the name the tester has assigned each picture, which is not obvious. *Cub* is a bear, *plate* is a purple patterned oval, *doughnut* is black with yellow on top (perhaps icing, or is it a bagel with cheese on it?). In another set, a picture of a two-inch yellow grasshopper is named *insect*. Then the child must understand that when the tester says, "Which picture begins with /d/?" the question really is, "Which word that names the picture begins with that sound?" Now the child must recall each picture name and abstract, from what he or she remembers hearing, the beginning sound or sounds, since the scoring accepts more than a single first sound. Finally, the child must identify or say that sound in isolation from the word.

This case of multiple but irrelevant opportunities for the child to produce an incorrect response is a good example of the old adage, "There's many a slip twixt the cup and the lip." If a picture looks like a bear, will the child remember that the tester called it a cub? If the doughnut looks like a bagel with cheese on it, will the child think *doughnut*? If the child is already reading and knows that *cub* starts with the letter *c*, will he or she be less likely to identify the picture as starting with the /k/ sound? Is the plate a dish?

So what looks like an easy task turns out to be very complex. The concept of phonemic awareness, which the ISF subtest claims to be testing, is that children need to be able to abstract sounds out of words to be able to read. But haven't children already shown in learning to speak the language that they control how sounds come together in producing words? So why use a complex task designed to get children to show they can abstract an initial sound from a word?

Wouldn't it be simpler for the tester to say a word and the child to respond with the beginning sound (as happens in Phoneme Segmentation Fluency [PSF])? The pictures seem to complicate the task more than they help, introducing several layers of abstraction quite unrelated to the goal of the testing.

Problems with Phoneme Segmentation Fluency (PSF)

PSF is also intended to test phonological (phonemic) awareness, but whereas the previous test only asks the child to abstract the initial sound from the word, this subtest requires the child to break "three and four phoneme words" into separate sounds.

While it is certainly more straightforward than the previous test, the PSF subtest requires a higher level of abstraction since each sound in the word must be separated, whereas in the ISF subtest the child can say the initial sound or the initial blend (*p* or *pl* for *plate*, for example). The DIBELS authors admit that it is difficult to produce a single phoneme in isolation and do accept consonants with neutral *schwa* vowels attached (e.g., *kuh* rather than *k*).

Older discussions divide phonics into synthetic and analytic phonics. PSF is a test of analytic phonics, as is ISF: Children are asked to analyze the constituent sounds in a given oral word. In synthetic phonics sounds are blended to produce, or synthesize, words. This is not so much then a test of phonemic or phonological awareness as it is a test of analytic phonics, or the ability to break words into component sounds.

What Is Phonics? The DIBELS authors believe that the ability to abstract sounds from words is a necessary prerequisite to reading. In *Phonics Phacts* (Goodman 1993), I demonstrate that phonics is the ability to relate the spelling patterns of English to the sound patterns of someone's speech. Since each of us speaks a dialect of English, these relationships vary from dialect to dialect. The child's task in the PSF subtest is to hear a spoken word (in the dialect of the tester) and abstract from what he or she perceives—that is, what he or she thinks was heard—the component sounds. For example, if the tester says "when," which the score sheet says is composed of three sounds, *w, e, n,* but the child pronounces the word as *hwen* (most Southerners do) and hears four sounds, then the child would be marked wrong.

Given the choice of the twenty-four words in both the kindergarten and first grade benchmark tests, it is clear that the DIBELS authors have little understanding of the nature of English phonics. They clearly are wrong on some words in what should be expected and clearly are unaware of dialect difference in other word choices. The words that the children are asked to break into sounds appear to be random; considering this is a subtest to be administered to kindergarten and first grade children, there could be too many unplanned responses which are likely to be scored as incorrect.

Long Vowels What are commonly called *long vowels* in English are actually composed of short vowels and glides. The *long*

E in these words from the kindergarten benchmark PSF subtest means that *seem, key,* and *ear* are all /iy/. Long *I* is actually /oy/ as in *guy* and *by.* Long *A* is /ey/ as in *taste.* There is also a /w/ glide in English, as in *crowd, shout,* and *loud.* The authors recognize this glide but they expect the children to hear the vowel plus glide /ow/ as a single sound.

Many decades of research on how children perceive sounds in the speech they hear shows that children often hear subtle sound differences that literate adults tune out. So children are likely to hear two sounds—vowel and glide—in these words. One child writing the word *make* put an *h* at the end after the *k.* Actually there is an aspiration there. Another child commented that *p* and *b* "are both with the lips."

Open O   Phonologists recognize that there is an *o* sound that they call the *open O,* which is neither short nor long in most American English dialects. The kindergarten benchmark form of the PSF subtest has the word *ought.* Some people say *ought* to rhyme with *cot,* and indeed the score sheet counts that as correct. But more Americans would rhyme it with words like *taught, bought,* and *sought,* which use the open O. The authors expect *cause* to have a short O but again it is more often an open O. Only a few American children would say *hawk* the same as *hock* but that is the right answer in this subtest.

Nasalization   In words like *stand* and *meant,* the *t* and *d* tend to be lost after the nasal sound, so children might not hear these sounds.

Scoring   There are two related problems in scoring the PSF subtest. One problem is dialect variations, as I've pointed out above. Since phonics is matching the spelling patterns of English with a speaker's sound patterns, it is very much dependent on dialect differences. In this subtest it is particularly likely that testers will not accept dialect and articulation responses since they would have to reconstruct how the child would have said the word. In one form of the PSF subtest the words *row, your,* and *more* occur. Will the testers accept that for some dialects these are rhyming words with the same vowel and no final /r/? Will they accept that some New York children might hear a /g/ at the end of *hung?*

Will they understand that children from the South hear *pine* as having the same vowel as *pond*? This is complicated by the subtest authors who are in error in several cases on what sounds to expect.

The second problem is that it is hard for even professional phonologists and dialecticians to be sure what speech sounds they hear in oral speech. They rely on recording and acoustic instruments. Testers in this subtest must judge the sounds they hear in a few seconds as they are hearing them with no record to replay. So its highly unlikely that any child could get a fair hearing, that there could be inter-tester reliability, or that the same tester would be consistent across different children.

So what instruction will children get who don't achieve benchmarks? Will children penalized for their dialect be subjected to intensive instruction on how to produce sounds that don't match their dialect? Will such instruction inhibit or further their reading development?

Problems with Nonsense Word Fluency (NWF)

The authors claim to be testing the "alphabetic principle," which I assume means that there are relationships between letters and sounds. The children are told that they are to read "make-believe words" as best they can. They may either point to each letter and say the sound or read the whole word. They get one point for each correct sound whether they read each as a nonsense word or letter by letter.

In constructing several stories using nonsense words to illustrate the use of the cuing systems in making sense of print, I've learned that it is not an easy task to create nonsense words that are both pronounceable and possible in terms of English spelling rules. In one story

> **Note from a teacher**
>
> I found that the nonsense words confused more able readers. Thankfully, my children have been conditioned to expect written language to convey meaning or message. Typically, my able students were able to read more of the words but encountered more difficulty, particularly with words that closely resemble real words. For example, when coming upon *lik*, it was as if they were thinking to themselves, "Well, that is not lick, because I KNOW how to write lick. That word could be *like*, lots of kids write it that way . . ." and sure enough, they mispronounced these words in an attempt to make some sort of sense out of the ridiculous.

I used what I thought was a nonsense word that turned out to be an obscenity in Australia. In another case I ended a word with *v* and discovered that English words cannot end in *v*. The only hint that the authors provide in the DIBELS manual to the rules they used for constructing their nonsense words is that they have not used *x* and *q*; used *h, w, y*, and *r* only in initial position; and used *c* and *g* only in final position. Since they think they are only testing the ability to match letters and sounds, I assume they think they have thus created nonsense words where these relationships are one-to-one, which of course is a distortion of the alphabetic principle in English since letters and letter combinations can in fact represent different sounds, and vice versa. They use only monosyllables probably to avoid long vowels and schwa in unaccented syllables.

An examination of just one form of the test sheets the children are asked to respond to reveals several problems common to all the alternate forms with the so-called make-believe words.

Words That Are Real Words and Not Nonsense This page of the NWF subtest contains these real English words: *wan, tam, mum*. Children who are already readers are likely to read them as they are pronounced in their particular dialect and thus risk been scored wrong. In other forms of this subtest, real Spanish words such as *los, el, es*, and *dos* are included. That makes second language pupils likely to be misscored for using Spanish phonemes. For the many American children whose first language is Spanish, some words beginning with *j* are likely to get an /h/ sound. On this page, *juj, juf, jev*, and *jup* are included. Those children would also be likely to produce Spanish vowel sounds. The testers could count Spanish pronunciations as correct if they were sensitive to this issue but that, at best, would be inconsistent. Of course other children whose home language is not English would also tend to be penalized for mispronunciations.

Words That Are Actually Possible English Spellings for Real English Words These are very common in the NWF subtest. The words look much like the common invented spellings of children in these grades who use their knowledge of the alphabetic principle to invent spellings. So they will read these words as the real words in their own dialect. *Ironically then, children who use the alphabetic principle to invent spellings will be scored lower in a test that claims to test the alphabetic principle.*

In this page are found *yiz* (a perfectly good word in New Jersey), *ful, mik, zum, nuf, kun, fod, vep, juj, sug, ov, wam, buk, lef, luk, lof, kom, nol, rez* (a good word in the Southwest), *poz, ol, kav, kic, kis, tek, riz, aj, vej, som, zuz.*

Words That Violate English Spelling Rules   Several words in the NWF subtest end in *j: ij, juj,* and *vej.* If the children are only matching letters and sounds this may be only a minor problem—they'll be slowed down in their response by their surprise at the strange-looking pattern. But if they are already reading they will have a strong tendency to try to make sense of these items and may actually waste time commenting on how funny they look. Also, rare or non-existent in English are words ending in *ec* and *oc,* so *kec* and *zoc* are not possible spellings (*spec* and *rec* are abbreviations). Several items end in *z.* That sound at the end of words is usually spelled in English with an *s* or a double *z.* So the more the children know about English spelling the less well they are likely to do.

> **Note from a teacher**
>
> An important part of this issue is the consideration of what I did not use to assess my children this year. Previously, we used a set of assessments modeled on the work of Marie Clay, which I felt armed me with solid information for making sound instructional decisions. I did not assess phonemic awareness through a child's ability to encode from dictation. I did not get a measure of known words through the ten-minute word write from the OS Survey. I could not analyze these to see who is using generative strategies to write words, how children organize their thinking by writing through categories, who is taking chances with multisyllable words, who understands how to add suffixes and prefixes to known bases. . . . I missed all of that because I administered a nonsense word test.

Words That Look Like Real Words   Several words on the NWF subtest look enough like real English words that children may be led to respond with those words: *ful (full), mik (Mike, milk), fod (food), wam (warm), lof (loaf), tam (tame), pum (plum), ut (but), som (some), jup (jump).*

So many problems with the so-called make-believe words in which the children must match letters with sounds surely means that there is little likelihood that the authors are testing what they think they are testing in any useful way and that the scores have any meaning.

The authors acknowledge that those who say the whole word save time and therefore will achieve higher scores in the one-minute test. On the other hand, those trying to make sense of nonsense may actually do less well than those who use the separate sound strategy since they will be producing real words in their own dialects and not ones that match the testers' expectations.

And what kind of intensive instruction will those not making the benchmark scores receive to improve their performance? The message will be, "Forget about making sense and just try to say the sounds correctly, no matter how funny that sounds to you." This can hardly be construed as progress toward reading competence.

> **Note from a teacher**
>
> I don't know how the testing can be done consistently. From my work as a Reading Recovery teacher I know that it takes some time to train your ear to hear what a child is reading/saying with words or with extended text. Teachers with no experience were thrust into this situation.

Scoring this test fairly requires great sensitivity to issues of articulation, dialect, and second-language variation in speech sounds, which means some children's scores will suffer more than others.

Problems with Oral Reading Fluency (ORF) and Retell Fluency (RF)

In ORF, the pupils' task is to read out loud "connected text" accurately and rapidly. The score is the number of right words read in one minute. Wrong words are those omitted, substituted, or where the reader hesitates three seconds. Insertions are not counted. For unexplained reasons the test is repeated for three different passages and the middle score is the one that is counted. I can only assume that the authors think they are making up for what they believe may be unintentional differences in passage difficulty.

Choice of Passages   The passages appear to have been written expressly for the test. The first grade passages are about 215 words long. The second grade ones are about 240 words. Third

grade passages are about 260 words. Each has the form of a four-
or five-paragraph essay rather than a story. Almost all are in first
person. Here's the beginning of one passage from first grade:

> Our kitten was sick. She would not eat and she stopped drinking.
> She did not purr anymore. She wanted to sleep all the time. She
> cried if I touched her.

Here's the beginning of a third grade passage:

> I saw a show on TV last night about animal tracks. Animals and
> people leave their footprints, or tracks, wherever they go. Each
> track tells a story. A good tracker can tell what kind of animal
> made the tracks. For instance, members of the dog family have
> four toes on each foot. A tracker can see the toenail marks in the
> footprint of a dog. The dog family includes foxes, coyotes, and all
> pet dogs.

It's hard to see from the passages what principles were used in
constructing them. There is a sequence of statements around a
central topic but no plot and no setting or characterization. Since
the authors define reading competence as reading words rapidly
and correctly, they may not feel they needed to be concerned
about anything in the passage other than that it is indeed a connected text. That is consistent with their scoring, which for Oral
Reading Fluency is the number of correct words in one minute
and for Retell Fluency is the number words in the retelling before the child stops talking for five seconds or "gets off track."

Text Difficulty Teachers report that the passages used in the
ORF subtest are difficult for the level of children they are intended for. They also report that passages vary considerably in
difficulty within the same group of three to be administered in a
single session and that they often involve concepts outside the
experience of their pupils.

There is an extensive professional literature on the nature of
texts of different genres and what make texts hard or easy. There
is also a good deal of research on oral reading of texts, including
several hundred studies that use miscue analysis, which focuses not
so much on correct responses but on the quality of miscues (unexpected responses) that always occur in any oral reading. There

is considerable evidence that readers can look more or less proficient in different texts depending on the type and quality of the text and the background the reader brings to the text. It may well be that the DIBELS authors stayed with the first-person essay to avoid the problem of how different types of texts effect reading performance. But by doing so they have reduced reading to the reading of a particular type of text and not a terribly common one. To the authors' credit, the passages are not "decodable" texts composed of consistent letter-sound relationships. The passages use English wording and syntax. But the passages are not very predictable since there are no plots or central theses to guide the reader to build meaning.

All this is likely to underrepresent the child looking for meaning in the passage and overrate the child concerned with saying only as many right words as possible.

Speed and Accuracy The authors see no need to measure anything in the reading of connected text except how many words a reader can read accurately in a minute. But in this they are assuming that the speed and accuracy of reading in the first minute of a reading is much the same as all minutes of reading. In fact a number of studies show that rate and accuracy vary considerably across a text. "Our kitten was sick" may take less time per word than "She cried if I touched her." The latter has a more complex syntax and fewer common words. The beginning of any text is usually a bit harder for the reader because it takes a reader a while to get used to the style and content. Furthermore, what is happening in the text strongly influences speed and accuracy.

> **Note from a teacher**
>
> I saw immediate negative carryover from this assessment, particularly among children reluctant to take chances. It seemed as though the assessment inadvertently gives children permission not to think about unknown words and reinforces those who play the waiting game, hoping someone will just tell them a word. It just plain seems to fly in the face of good literacy teaching.

The "Next Word" View of the Authors The tester times three-second hesitations, marks a word wrong, and tells the reader that word. That assumes that the pause is always because the reader doesn't know the next word in the line. But it is as likely that the reader knows the word but is trying to figure out how to make sense of it in this context. Take, for example, this line from the kitten passage: "the vet is an animal doctor." Suppose a reader pauses before *animal*—not because she doesn't know the word, but because "the vet is an animal" doesn't make sense. In three seconds, the tester says, "animal." In doing so the child gets the message that she is to say each word whether it makes sense or not. And a word that the child knew is counted wrong. In miscue research, we've learned that a reader may take much longer to solve this type of a problem—as much as thirty seconds—but when the problem is solved we see real evidence of problem solving and making progress in reading development. Of course, there's no time in a one-minute test for making sense of reading. Teachers report that pupils who quickly skip over less common words and just say the words they know do well on this subtest and can even rattle off a few words from the passage in their "retelling."

Quantity and Quality   DIBELS bases all judgment on quantitative scores. Within this they might have been more consistent within their own belief if the score on Oral Reading Fluency were the percentage of words that were read correctly or self-corrected rather than the number of correct words read. That would avoid rewarding speed for the sake of speed. But that requires a bit more sophistication on the part of the scorer.

The authors' belief that reading must be accurate leads them to pay no attention to the *quality* of the reading, that is, the extent to which the readers are making sense of (comprehending) what they are reading. That shows in the quality of miscues (unexpected responses). Do the readers keep the meaning even though they substitute synonyms or modify the syntax? Do they self-correct when they lose meaning? Do they get words later in the passage that they didn't earlier? These are questions DIBELS doesn't ask.

Scoring the Retelling   The scoring of the retelling is also a problem in this type of passage. A mature retelling of the kitten passage might be, "It was about a kitten," or "It was about somebody's cat getting sick." Another retelling might string phrases together to produce more words and get a higher score.

The Retelling Fluency (RF) subtest was added, according to the authors, as an optional additional task to satisfy teachers that the children understand what they read. But strangely, the RF score is limited to counting the words the child used in retelling. No attention is paid in scoring to how well the retelling represents the meaning of the passage. In most uses of retelling in assessing comprehension there is some probing beyond the initial free retell. Usually the examiner says, "Can you tell me anything else?" or "Tell me more about . . . ." Here the assumption is made that all that was understood is expressed in the initial response.

> **Note from a teacher**
>
> In our very large urban school district, teachers are required to group students for reading as a result of their DIBELS oral fluency score, not the even more ridiculous timed oral retell score which counts the number of words a student is able to spit back orally in one minute. After students are "grouped by their DIBELS score," we then must do a "Walk to Read." This is where all the lowest students are grouped with one teacher, and the higher students go off to another teacher. We are required to do this for ninety minutes every day. In addition, students who indicate they need "intensive intervention" must be pulled out of my classroom at another time in the day for additional reading "help."

Again, as in other subtests of DIBELS, if the children are rehearsed on reading fast and saying as much as they can about each passage as fast as they can, they will improve their score on this subtest. But it would be hard to see that as progress in reading competence.

Problems with Word Use Fluency (WUF)

The authors must consider this important because they want it tested from kindergarten through third grade even though it is presented as optional and no benchmarks are provided. They do provide estimated scores that would lead to intensive instruction. I assume that the subtest is intended to test vocabulary. The authors indicate that they are gathering data from scores reported to them in order to establish benchmarks. This raises an ethical issue. Do the authors have permission from the parents of the children to gather such research data? They apparently do not. This could cause legal problems for school districts.

Is It a Reading Test?   Since the task involves oral responses to a word read by the tester it does not appear to be an aspect of reading that is being tested but at most a test of productive oral vocabulary, which may or may not contribute to development of reading competence. Making sense of print involves receptive vocabulary.

What's a Word?   Almost all words in English have several different meanings and more common words have more meanings. English words also often may be used with different grammatical functions. Words also frequently collocate with other words (for example, *look* and *at*) So when the tester says a word out of any context and asks the child to use it, the child must deal with a great deal of ambiguity. The scoring gives credit for homophones (i.e., *bored* and *board*), but how consistent will testers be in realizing the meaning the child has in mind in a response?

What Does "Use the Word" Mean?   The scoring instructions allow for the child to interpret the instructions to include using the word in a statement, providing a definition of the word, or even saying something about the word without really using it. But "use the word" is likely to be misunderstood as an instruction. Children as they get older may have a better sense of what the instruction means, but that is not an indication of reading development.

Choice of Words   Since word frequency has been used in reading programs for many years one might have expected the words used in this subtest to move from common to less common words. But the words in the lists at each level appear to be random. Some frequent words on the list are harder to use than others. A kindergarten list includes *which* and *else*, for example. I'd expect most kindergartners to hear *witch* and use that rather than *which*, since the words are homophones in most American English dialects and *which* is more abstract.

Quantitative Scoring   Again the child gets credit not for the quality of the use made of the target word but for the numbers of words used in using the word. It is hard to think of any reason to believe that the longer the utterance produced in using words the richer the vocabulary or the better the child reads. But that is what

DIBELS would have us believe. Ironically, longer responses take more time so there seems to be a trade-off. A lot of short utterances produced in a minute and a few long ones will get about the same scores. The tester in scoring "on the fly" in this subtest is saying a word, judging whether the use of the word is appropriate, counting the words in the utterance produced by the child, and timing five seconds on a stop watch, all at the same time. That's not easy to manage and the skill of the tester will surely influence the score each child gets.

Change over Time   Since children in schools where DIBELS is administrated get plenty of practice with this strange test it would be hard to imagine that they would not get better at figuring out how to improve their scores on it, particularly if their teachers make clear to them that the object is to use a lot of words in their responses. But what would such improvement have to do with their reading?

DIBELS and Reading

So far I've focused on how DIBELS defines reading and reading development and how that view is represented in DIBELS and its subtests. I've critiqued what DIBELS intends to measure, what it does measure, and how well it does what it intends to do. What it adds up to is that:

- DIBELS reduces reading to a few components that can be tested in one minute each.
- DIBELS does not test what it says it tests.
- What DIBELS does, it does poorly, even viewed from its own intentions and criteria.
- DIBELS cannot be administered and scored consistently.
- DIBELS does not test the quality of reading.
- Focus on improving performance on DIBELS is likely to contribute little or nothing to reading development and actually interfere with reading development.
- DIBELS misrepresents pupils.
- DIBELS demeans teachers.

So what does that add up to? *DIBELS is a set of silly little tests.* It is so bad in so many ways that it is hard to believe that it could have passed review for adoption in any state or district without political coercion being involved. The idea that one can learn anything useful about something as complicated as reading development in a series of one-minute tests is preposterous. One can't simplify something just by treating it as simple.

In this next section, I consider what is wrong with the basic premises of reading DIBELS and why its use is detrimental to reading development and effective instruction.

DIBELS is based on a view of reading as the ability to read words rapidly and accurately. In that view, comprehension is somehow the automatic result of this accurate and rapid word naming.

But reading is really making sense of written language. It is a constructive process in which the reader uses cues from the text to get to meaning. Reading needs to be both effective and efficient.

Effective reading is success in making sense of a written text, something which no part of DIBELS measures. Efficient reading is making sense using as little effort and energy as possible.

Efficient reading may appear to be rapid because the reader is selective in using cues from the text to get to meaning and does not attend to every detail of every letter in every word. *But speed is the result of efficiency and not a cause.* Research in miscue analysis has demonstrated this efficiency. Eye movement studies have shown that the reader's eye does not even fixate on about 30 percent of the words in a text. That's because the reader is constructing meaning and anticipating many of the words without needing to specifically identify them. If the reader loses meaning, then the reader may regress for more sampling of the text.

By focusing attention on accurate rapid responses to letters, sounds, nonsense, and words, in and out of context, DIBELS teaches inefficiency, makes readers less effective, and penalizes young pupils who are beginning to make sense of print.

Learning to read is not learned from part to whole, as DIBELS assumes. Nor is it an invariant sequence of small stepping stones, each prerequisite to the next. Just as children learn to speak and understand oral language by being immersed in it, they need to be involved with real, meaningful, and whole texts right from the beginning.

Humans have a universal ability to create and learn language. If children have rich opportunities to read and write for real purposes they show remarkable ease in becoming readers and writers. DIBELS doesn't help teachers to provide these rich opportunities; it takes control from them and keeps them from using their professional judgment built through years of education and teaching experience.

How DIBELS Treats Children

Children are treated in DIBELS as interchangeable. Regardless of their experience, their maturity, or their cognitive and linguistic backgrounds, they must be passed through the same sequence of tests and the reasons why they perform the way they do on test tasks are not important; what counts is an arbitrary score. There is an assumption not only of a single learning sequence but also that all children become literate in the same way and that literacy is something only developed through instruction.

Yet studies by Yetta Goodman, Emilia Ferreiro, Marie Clay, and many others show that children begin making sense of print in their environment and playing at writing long before they start school, and they show this in many ways that can be easily observed but are concealed in the subtests of DIBELS.

How DIBELS Treats Teachers

"The reading wars are over and we all know who won." This is how the principal trainer in one urban district starts her DIBELS training. So teachers are prisoners of war. Teachers are treated by DIBELS as interchangeable. The authors of DIBELS believe they know better than the most experienced teachers what instruction a given child or group of children need at any point in time. Teachers become untrustworthy technicians who must deliver "intensive instruction" to children according to reports received from a computer in Oregon.

Essentially teachers are being told that a series of one-minute tests are so scientific that they as professionals may not vary their use or even question the tests. Knowledgeable and experienced teachers who have known how bad DIBELS is have been forced to sit in silence and punished for asking questions while they have been "trained" to use DIBELS.

What Parents Need to Understand About DIBELS

At best, DIBELS takes control of the most important relationship a child has outside his home—the relationship with his or her teacher. The teacher is forced to substitute scores on timed tests for professional, compassionate judgment. At its worst, DIBELS takes control of the entire school experience a child has from the first day of kindergarten (or even preschool in some cases) through third grade and beyond. Three times a year children are tested with benchmark DIBELS tests. Once a month their progress is monitored with DIBELS tests. Children who miss the benchmarks are tested more frequently. And in between? They practice for the test! There's no time for anything else— art, science, social studies, music, recess—only a little math done in the same stressful way as reading.

And ironically there is precious little time for really reading stories and real books. The children are too busy learning to do what the tests test than to have time to read. And DIBELS does not test reading. It doesn't even test what it claims it tests, the so-called stepping stones to reading.

The continuous use of timed tests puts young children under totally unnecessary stress. And parents can easily see the signs of this stress, particularly on the all too frequent test days—sleeplessness, resistance to going to school, bed-wetting, and the rest.

If teachers want to rely on their own experience and the knowledge they build of each individual child in their rooms, they are told they cannot vary how they use the test or the instruction its manual mandates. That forces highly effective teachers to make hard choices: leave teaching, move to a higher grade, or even cheat on behalf of the children.

If parents doubt that what their children face with DIBELS is as bad as I and the teachers I've quoted say it is, you can see for yourselves: Download DIBELS from the website. Visit your child's school. Ask for an appointment with the teacher and/or the principal of the school. You may also find that the school has a DIBELS "cop" to keep the teachers in line. And don't be surprised if you ask why they are using DIBELS the answer is, "They're making us do it." Who are they? The feds, the state, the school board?

A Word on Statistics

In the DIBELS manual the authors present statistical data purporting to show the relationships of each of the DIBELS subtests to various other tests of reading. Other critics have carefully checked out the research claims DIBELS authors make and find few studies reported in respected journals. I have not checked their claims and will grant for the purpose of discussion that their claims are true. I do challenge however that these correlational claims prove anything about the quality of DIBELS and the uses being made of it. There are several reasons for my view:

1. All tests correlate with all other tests. Tests of math for instance will correlate with reading tests. There is a test-taking factor that cuts across tests regardless of design or content.
2. As reading ability (defined as the ability to make sense of print) increases, children will eventually do better on all tests that involve reading and writing.
3. Correlations do not show cause-effect relationships. In the case of the Oral Reading Fluency subtest, which involves the number of words that can be read accurately in one minute, it is more likely that being able to make sense of print leads to speed and accuracy than that speed and accuracy lead to making sense.
4. Several subtests are more tests of the ability to deal with abstraction than of reading. These include Letter Naming Fluency, Initial Sound Fluency, Phonemic Segmentation Fluency, Nonsense Word Fluency, and Word Use Fluency. This ability to

deal with abstraction is also a factor in other tests in more and less obvious ways.

5. Factors such as inconsistent scoring and potential for cheating make any statistics derived from the data highly suspect.

6. Since each subtest is given frequently and there is intensive practice for the test, there is a practice effect that can produce statistical progress that does not reflect reading progress.

Science, Technology, and DIBELS

When a teacher in rural New Mexico inputs pupil scores on DIBELS subtests into a Palm Pilot and those scores are electronically transmitted to the state Department of Education and then to a computer in Oregon, it can appear that another miracle of modern science is being witnessed. When the same teacher gets back a computer-generated report with a list of names of specific children that need intensive instruction in Letter Naming Fluency or Nonsense Word Fluency, it may seem that compliance with what science has determined is right for each of these children will assure that they will one day become competent readers.

But technology and science are not the same thing. The data that goes into the DIBELS computer is the result of badly constructed tests that reduce what the authors believe are Big Ideas of reading—defined as rapid accurate word naming—to tasks in which responses can be counted in one minute. Furthermore, the scores that are input are unreliable, inconsistent, and capricious depending on the tester and on the child's understanding of the tasks. On top of that, with stakes so high and access to the tests so easy, the possibilities of cheating at a number of different levels make the input scores highly questionable anyway. The principle in computer technology is garbage in, garbage out.

DIBELS and the Pedagogy of the Absurd

Elsewhere I have argued that this period in American Education will be characterized as the pedagogy of the absurd.

Nothing better illustrates this than DIBELS. It is an absurd set of silly little one-minute tests that never get close to measuring what reading is really about—making sense of print. It is absurd that politicians in Washington and state boards and Departments of Education have forced it on thousands of schools and millions of children. It is absurd that scores on these silly little tests are used to judge schools, teachers, and children. It is absurd that use of DIBELS has turned kindergartens into basic training for test-driven primary education And it is a tragedy that life decisions are being made for five- and six-year-olds on the basis of such absurd criteria.

References

Goodman, Kenneth S. 1993. *Phonics Phacts*. Portsmouth, NH: Heinemann.

Kauerz, Kristie. 2005. "State Kindergarten Policies: Straddling Early Learning and Early Elementary School." *Young Children* (March) 60 (2).

Manzo, Kathleen Kennedy. 2005. "Publishers question fairness of Reading First Process." *Education Week* (September 7) 25 (02): 24.

Manzo, Kathleen Kennedy. 2005. "National Clout of DIBELS Test Draws Scrutiny." *Education Week* (September 28) 25 (5): 1, 12.

National Reading Panel. 2000. *Teaching Children to Read: An evidence-based assessment of the scientific research literature on reading and its implications for reading instruction*. Washington DC: U.S. Department of Health and Human Services, National Institute of Child Health and Human Development.

What's "Normal" About Real Reading?

Alan Flurkey
Hofstra University

Justin

"Justin" is an eight-year-old boy who is in my second-grade class. He was held back last year and attended summer school based on his DIBELS results. As of spring 2005 Justin's Oral Reading Fluency was 42 words per minute (wpm).

The students are tested only on Oral Reading Fluency (ORF) and Nonsense Word Fluency (NWF). Although there is a Retell Fluency (RTF) section on DIBELS we are not required to administer it. In our school we are told that these results have a dire impact on whether a student will be promoted to the next grade. We are a Reading First school. Our Reading First coaches state, "Research shows that fluency has a direct impact on a child's ability to comprehend accurately."

During summer school the DIBELS assessment was implemented weekly. Justin's fluency was tested and retested a number of times. Each time his results read High Risk due to his lack of fluency, although when you take a closer look his reading accuracy ranged from 62 percent to 99 percent. Miscues were highlighted but not recorded. (By looking at DIBELS data we only know that he either omitted or substituted the word, not what he actually said.)

Justin's DIBELS results are much different this year. According to his results he has reached the Low Risk marker. This means for this assessment he reached the designated benchmark number of words per minute (beginning grade 2, 44 wpm, and the middle of grade 2, 68 wpm). I believe that Justin is meeting these benchmarks because he is now reading these passages for the second time, having an advantage over the other students who have not. For students to meet the benchmark and be promoted to third grade they must meet the 90 ORF benchmark for end of year.

I believe Justin is an average reader; however, his mother is hung up on concerns raised by a previous teacher. Even though his reading is not as "fluent" as other students in my class he has extremely strong comprehension skills.

This story was recently told to me by a teacher in a Long Island school district. Stories like this are deeply troubling because a major educational decision is based on a flawed test. And the tragedy is that the test is based on a flawed view of reading. It is important to note that even though this child's reading may not meet the benchmark on the DIBELS test, the child is still reading and he understands what he reads. It may even be that this reader, who is learning to control reading *flexibly*, is penalized for doing what is "normal" in reading.

But just what *is* normal in reading? And what does it mean for reading to be flexible? For one thing, *thinking* is normal in reading, and thinking takes time. And readers are flexible when they read. They continually speed up and slow down, monitoring their understanding, as they make sense of what they're reading. Sometimes, when a stretch of text is predictable and the sense-making seems effortless, readers speed up and process text relatively quickly. And sometimes, when what readers encounter doesn't quite fit with their initial expectations, readers may need to proceed more slowly and tentatively, and may pause to think about how to make sense of what they're reading, or repeat words or phrases that they've just read in order to better understand what they are reading.

But in every case, readers do not read with complete accuracy. They don't read with complete accuracy when the sense-making seems effortless, and they don't read with complete accuracy when they are proceeding slowly and tentatively. And this is true of both mature, proficient readers *and* of young readers who are just coming to control the process of reading.

In other words, it's *normal* for readers to not read with complete accuracy as they go about making sense as they read. But this view of reading, which has been described and explored in hundreds of studies of miscue analysis (Brown, Goodman, and Marek 1996) runs counter to the view that is reflected in the DIBELS assessments.

A Machine View of Reading

In a link to the DIBELS official website, labeled "Accuracy and Fluency" (http://reading.uoregon.edu/flu/flu_what_2.php), the literature claims that research says that proficient readers rapidly and accurately identify words. Rapid, automatic, accurate word recognition is thought to be a necessary skill so that readers can then use their attention to comprehend what they read. Furthermore, it is thought that "It is not enough to be simply accurate; the skill must be automatic" (Hasbrouck, Ihnot, and Rogers 1999; Moats 1999).

But how accurate is this machine view of reading? An uninterrupted tape recording of an oral reading of a whole story tells a different story. Consider the following reading (Figure 1) of the first pages of the children's book *Blueberries for Sal* (McCloskey 1976). The reader's responses are written in above the text; © indicates that the reader has self-corrected a response, circled words indicate omissions, and ^ indicates words the reader has inserted.

In this observation, the reader does not appear to be accurately identifying words, so one might question whether or not the reading is "automatic" and whether or not the reader had sufficient attention to apply to comprehension of the story. Indeed, one might wonder whether or not this is a skilled reader reading this story. But on closer inspection, note that all of the reader's responses either make sense or represent reasonable predictions that are then corrected. For example, the text says:

> Then she ate more berries and dropped one in the pail—*kerplunk!*
> And the rest she ate.

The reader's version:

> Then she ate some more berries and dropped them in the pail—
> *kerplink!*
> And she ate the rest.

Blueberries for Sal
By Robert McCloskey

One day, Little Sal ⓒ *and* went with her mother to Blueberry

Hill to pick *some* blueberries.

Little Sal brought *along* her small tin pail and her

mother brought her large tin pail to put berries in. "We

will take our berries home and can them," said her mother.

"Then we will have ⓒ *them* food for the winter."

Little Sal picked three berries and dropped them in her

little tin pail...kuplink, kuplank, kuplunk!

She picked three more berries and ate them. Then she

picked *some* more berries and dropped *them* one in the pail ⓒ *kuplink* kuplunk!

And the rest she ate. Then Little Sal ate all four (blue-)

berries out of her pail!

Her mother walked slowly through the bushes, picking

blueberries as she went and ⓒ *put* putting them *into* in her pail. Little Sal

struggled along behind, picking blueberries and eating every single

one.

Little Bear followed behind his mother as she walked

slowly through the bushes eating *blue* berries.

Then he had to ⓒ *hurry* hustle along to catch up!

Because his feet were tired of hustling, he picked out a large clump

of bushes and sat *right down* down right in the middle and ate blueberries.

Figure 1 *Marked typescript of* Blueberries for Sal

The reader's responses do not seem to disrupt the meaning of the story. But even though the two versions, the printed text and the reader's oral reading, are parallel, the reader has produced twelve incorrect responses in the first one hundred words of the story. Three of the twelve responses were corrected, leaving nine incorrect responses. So is this reader "at risk"? Not likely. The reader is a proficient adult who is a director of an investment banking firm in New York City. The reading shown here was discreetly tape-recorded while the reader was reading a bedtime story to his daughter. The responses observed are normal and provide a portrait of the reader's personal construction of meaning and the reader's concern for making sense as he reads. For real reading, this *is* normal.

A Meaning Construction View of Reading

Studies of oral reading have shown that readers are continually constructing personal meanings and monitoring their understandings of what they read *as they read* (Brown, Goodman, and Marek 1996). These two principles account for readers' unexpected responses to text. In the previous example, the principles account for the adult reader's meaningful substitutions, omissions, insertions, and corrections. In fact, these kinds of responses are so common among proficient readers of every age and experience that I call them "garden variety miscues." And these insights that come from studies of readers' uninterrupted oral reading of real texts raise an important question: Shouldn't we know how the reading process works for proficient readers in natural settings before we take steps to correct readers' mistakes? That question frames my critique of the DIBELS model of assessment—assessment that highlights so-called deficits and then points the way to forms of instruction that may not support the development of reading for meaning among young children.

Taking Time to Read

Much is made about the importance of readers' automatic responses to the printed matter in the DIBELS subtests. Readers are penalized for taking too much time to accomplish the tasks they are given. But again, observations of readers reading whole texts tell a different story. Figure 2 shows an excerpt of a third-grader orally reading a folktale. The reader read the entire story at a rate of only 44 words per minute. Yet during the reading, there were several instances of pauses and repetitions, responses that are the result of using strategies that take time to employ.

Note that the reading rate varies from sentence to sentence as the reader encounters various syntactic and semantic features in the text. Sometimes she solves the puzzle by rereading and correcting her initial predictions as she did in sentences 32 and 33. But sometimes, as in sentence 34, she seems to accept that she is puzzled and simply moves on. For example, in sentence 34 she produces a long twenty-three-second pause before continuing to read. Although she can identify the words in the story, it's not the *words* that are making her think in this instance—it's the meaning of the unfamiliar phrase *keeping house* that has this third-grader puzzled. She seems to be thinking, "How do you *keep* a *house*?" The reader's rate varies substantially from the overall 44 word per minute rate because she is thinking about what she is reading as she constructs meaning.

In addition, it is essential to recognize that the reader completely understood what she was reading as demonstrated by her detailed retelling of the story. The markings in Figure 2 show *where* she took time to make sense of the story, and by closely scrutinizing her responses we can make some good inferences about *why* she took the time she did. It seems to be all part of what was necessary for this reader to construct meaning for herself. And although she does not display responses we would expect in an *efficient* reading, she nonetheless produces an *effective* reading of this story.

Reading Flow

The metaphor of *flow*, which is predicated on a meaning construction view of reading, seems to provide a better fit of observations of readers reading whole texts than does *fluency*, a construct that is underpinned by a machine view of reading. *Flow* refers to the way

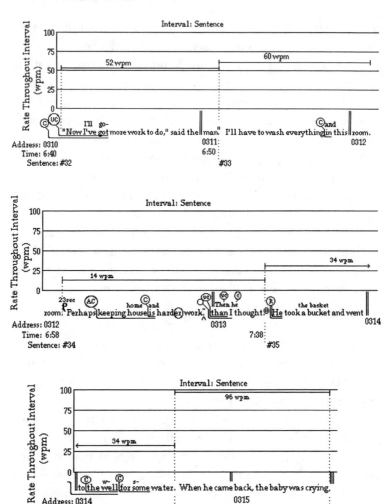

Figure 2 *Varied oral reading rates*

that reading rate continually speeds up and slows down as readers construct meaning. Figure 3 illustrates this idea. In Figure 3, the sentence reading rates are juxtaposed next to one another for each of the sixty-eight sentences in the folktale *The Man Who Kept House* (1962). The chart on the left shows the sentence rates for a proficient reading produced by a seventh grader. The chart on the right shows the sentence rates for the same third grader whose effective (but not efficient) reading was shown in Figure 2.

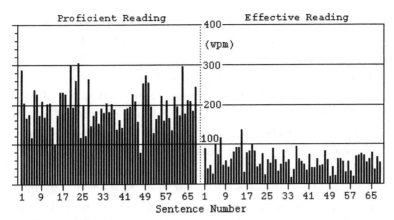

Proficient Reading Rate = 181 wpm over entire text
Effective Reading Rate = 44 wpm over entire text

Figure 3 *Consecutive Sentence Reading Rates for a Proficient Reading by a Seventh Grader and an Effective Reading by a Third Grader*

A stair-stepped contour is displayed in both readings. The figure shows that readers are continually speeding up and slowing down as they respond to the text. It also bears mentioning that the proficient reading was by no means error free. The seventh-grade reader produced a handful of unexpected responses, some that were not corrected and some that were. The reader also produced a few brief, infrequent pauses, some in the same places as the less proficient reading.

It appears that both readers are doing the same things: speeding up and slowing down as they encounter conditions in the text that require time to think as they go about making sense. That's normal in reading. The difference between the two is that a proficient reader displays greater flexibility. Readers who display mature control over use of the reading process when transacting with a particular text are able to efficiently and flexibly control their use of the cognitive reading strategies of sampling, predicting, inferring, and confirming. When readers produce proficient readings, they display greater facility by speeding up when they *can* and by slowing down when they *need to.* Their control enables them to do whatever they deem necessary to identify and solve problems as they construct meaning.

Visualize reading flow as a toy boat in a small stream responding to the varied conditions of the streambed beneath the water. The boat slows down as it crosses wide pools or when it comes up to obstructions caused by debris. The boat might speed up as the stream narrows or as it crosses cataracts or rapids. Like a toy boat in a stream, so readers respond to the "riverbed" of text as they read. Readers may encounter syntactic logjams or semantic chutes. One can envision places in texts where readers encounter thought-provoking concepts, like wide pools where they must slow down and ponder the meaning of the text, and other stretches where the text-riverbed narrows and seems quite predictable. And the reader just moves along until the text-riverbed conditions change again.

A word-identification, machine view of *fluency* conjures an image of water flowing through a pipe at the same rate at all points along the course. This metaphor does not seem to fit observations of readings of whole texts, whereas a fine-grained study of readers reading whole texts shows that readers are continually speeding up and slowing down, pondering and thinking and proceeding more efficiently when sense-making seems effortless (Flurkey 1997). That is what's normal about reading.

I would ask important questions of those who look to implement an assessment system like DIBELS. Shouldn't we know how the reading process "normally" works before we intervene? Shouldn't we know that readers need time to think as they read before we insist on rapid and automatic responses? An insistence on rapid, accurate, and automatic responses to text might be counterproductive and result in sending unintended messages to the reader—that saying words correctly is more important than understanding what is read.

Readers are thinkers. When people read, they use their life experiences and what they know about language as they formulate expectations about what they seek to understand. The result is that readers' expectations and perceptions cause them to see what they think they will see, and make ample use of time as they do so. But when it comes to real reading, that's just normal.

References

Brown, J., K. Goodman, and A. Marek. 1996. *Studies in Miscue Analysis: An Annotated Bibliography*. Newark, DE: International Reading Association.

Flurkey, A. 1997. Reading as Flow: A Linguistic Alternative to Fluency. Unpublished doctoral dissertation. Tucson, AZ: University of Arizona.

Hasbrouck, J. E., C. Ihnot, and. G. H. Rogers. 1999. "'Read Naturally': A Strategy to Increase Oral Reading Fluency." *Reading Research and Instruction* 39 (1): 27–18.

McCloskey, R. 1976. *Blueberries for Sal*. New York: Viking Press.

McInnes, J. (Ed.). 1962. "The Man Who Kept House." *Magic and Make-Believe* (pp. 282–287). Canada: Thomas Nelson & Sons (Canada) Limited.

Moats, L. C. 1999. *Teaching Reading Is Rocket Science: What Expert Teachers of Reading Should Know and Be Able To Do*. Washington, DC: American Federation of Teachers.

Is DIBELS Leading Us Down the Wrong Path?

Robert J. Tierney, Dean
College of Education
University of British Columbia
and Catherine Thome
Principal Staff Development Coordinator,
Lake County Regional Office of Education

Introduction

There may have been gains in student performance arising from some of the Reading First initiatives and accountability regimens such as the Dynamic Indicators of Basic Early Literacy Skills (DIBELS) may be part of such pursuits, but we question whether the gains are more illusion than real and whether the impact of this testing program is worth the price in terms of narrowing the definition of literacy, literacy development, and teacher professionalism.

Some Context

The context for DIBELS is tied to federal policies, which were implemented by the United States Congress in an attempt to pursue a war against illiteracy and demands for accountability. Valid or not, the perception of declines in literacy and the arguable critique of child-centered approaches as responsible were perpetuated and used to justify unprecedented mandates tied to literacy reform efforts by the federal government and state and local education agencies. These mandates ranged from determinations of what can count as evidence to the formulation of a plan of action by a carefully selected National Reading Panel (NRP) to the No Child Left Behind (NCLB) legislation, which included initiatives such as Reading First. Implementation often included strong recommendations by federal funders to pursue certain interventions and selected assessment systems such as DIBELS.

A key dimension of the current reform efforts is the questionable link between testing, accountability, and student learning. There is widespread concern now that such assessments do not contribute positively to the achievement improvements that they tout (Nichols and Berliner 2005; Nichols, Glass, and Berliner 2005). Another dimension has been the imposition of narrowly based interventions for teaching reading emanating from the NRP's attempt at a synthesis, especially when the evidence, according to some panel members, was neither inclusive nor conclusive.

While the federal policy makers narrowed what might count as evidence, concerns were raised about what were to be considered key components of literacy. The NRP identified five essential components for reading success: phonemic awareness, phonics, vocabulary, fluency, and comprehension. These components became the defining elements of what comprised a "scientifically based" reading program. Literacy researchers questioned the narrowing of research that might inform practice. It should come as no surprise then that the assessment requirements for Reading First participation would mirror those same elements. Enter DIBELS, which coincidentally promises to measure just those elements.

Granted, DIBELS may not be the perpetrator of the reform system that was created nor the leaps of faith that were invited, but it certainly should be regarded as a major tool in these developments (House 1991). Without acknowledging the limitations of the evidence from the NRP and the problems with implementing a testing regimen tied to these element, DIBELS was developed to screen, monitor, and assess outcomes of the elements extrapolated from the NRP report.

The test developers suggest that DIBELS can be used as a means of screening students to identify those who are at risk, to monitor progress in selected areas for instructional emphasis, and to measure the outcome of a student's progress as a reader. In so doing, DIBELS links the means with the ends—in particular, by suggesting that it can be used to repeatedly assess student literacy development and also serve as a measure of outcomes. A key question for users of DIBELS is not whether repeated use of DIBELS improves performance on DIBELS, but whether or not it improves literacy performance and the advancement of literacies in society. By using DIBELS to screen students, to monitor progress, and to measure outcomes, DIBELS fails to separate outcomes from means.

Accordingly, what DIBELS measures and what teachers teach become the same. A number of problems can occur as a result. The DIBELS tests define what is taught and the outcomes that are measured, so that progress may not be much more than what was tested and taught. In other words, students may be performing better on tests (phonemic awareness, phonics, vocabulary, fluency, retelling) but not in terms of larger goals for literacy: expanded uses of various literacies to serve a range of purposes. DIBELS proponents seem to have fallen prey to believing that what they propose as treatments and measure are the same as literacy development. We know that students can learn what we directly teach them, but we would suggest that our goal is to achieve more and have measures that go beyond what we have taught directly. DIBELS falls short of what a measure of literacy progress should be.

DIBELS and Literacies

Pearson (2002) has argued that the role of research and teacher assessments is to expand rather than limit the tools that teachers might use. DIBELS does not enhance teachers' knowledge of student literacies in a manner that supports the full range of their literacy development. Whereas elsewhere in the world we are seeing the embrace of the new literacies—critical literacies and digital literacies—by mandating DIBELS the U.S. seems stalled on notions of literacy more aligned with thinking of the early 1960s.

The question one must ask is whether or not DIBELS fosters an enriched definition of literacy. Will DIBELS perpetuate notions of literacy out of sync with notions of new literacies and multiple literacies? When tests restrict and constrain teachers' expectations, goals, and practices, literacy becomes test scores. And, with the increased emphasis upon accountability with tests such as DIBELS, many teachers retreat to teaching what is testable. And what is testable seems tied to traditional teaching objectives rather than the new literacies, including multimodal and media-based learning technologies.

By focusing only on phonemic awareness, phonics, vocabulary, fluency, and comprehension, richer approaches to literacy have been diminished. Students' early oral language experiences, writing, and various other modes of representation, including dynamic forms of meaning making, have been pushed aside—even banned from the classroom.

We may be purging the literacies that students can and should engage with for notions of literacy and meaning making. Lewis and Fabos (2005) suggested that assessments such as DIBELS require teachers to "disregard the vitality of their pupils' literate lives and the needs they will have for their literate and social futures at home, at work, and in their communities" (498). DIBELS canonizes some forms of literacy and literacy elements and ignores others.

Indeed, DIBELS may be perpetuating the literacy gap it has promised to eliminate. By closely subscribing to only those five components defined as essential by the NRP and assessed by DIBELS, the definition of literacy has been narrowed for the most vulnerable students. For those school/districts who are neither high poverty nor low performing, children are less likely to be held to this narrow view of literacy. These children have a more balanced literacy environment that includes viewing, writing, and other critical literacies. Those children in schools receiving funding from Reading First are more likely to be restricted. Once again, the rich get richer and poor are left only with the most basic of the basics.

With NCLB and Reading First, teachers are facing increasing pressure to show student gains. If these teachers are pressured to focus on students' gains on DIBELS, then teaching to the test presents itself as a viable option. In the Nonsense Word Fluency (NWF) subtest, the idea is *not* to teach nonsense words, but to teach to what the DIBELS developers refer to as the Big Idea, which in this case is the alphabetic principle, or phonics. This hasn't stopped companies from marketing workbooks that teachers can use to teach nonsense words. Because of the pressure to improve students' decoding skills, administrators are buying and requiring the use of these marginal materials.

Teacher Professionalism

With DIBELS becoming the single benchmark, teachers are encouraged to observe and evaluate students through someone else's narrow lens. With the imposition of DIBELS, one begins to see the specter of comparison with peers, leading teachers to abandon what they know as good practice and to teach to the test. Even though teachers question how comprehension is narrowly tested through the DIBELS' Retell Fluency subtest, they are expected to teach and practice "comprehension" by doing fast literal retells. Yet comprehension is more than rapid retelling. Teachers should help students to be strategic, to develop strategies to monitor their own understanding. Teachers should be helping students to explore and deepen their understanding about what they've read, not seeing how many words they can say in a minute in retelling the text.

Many schools/districts require teachers to administer DIBELS, yet do nothing to facilitate the use of the data or more ideally prepare teachers to enlist a range of tools by which to assess their students. If the data are not being used to inform instruction, then the time required to assess students would better be used for instruction. Using "on the spot" information, teachers could be more proactive, rather than waiting until the results of posttesting show a child has not hit a benchmark. But with the focus firmly on achieving the benchmarks on the tests, teachers have no leeway in making instructional decisions. They can only drill their pupils to improve test performance.

Districts should be concerned with whether all teachers have developed the knowledge and skills to make good decisions regarding students' instructional needs. Do they have a sound understanding of the reading process and reading development whereby they have the basis to observe students and interpret and follow up their observations? Do they understand and can they use and adapt assessment practices (e.g., roaming the known, Running Records, interviews, think alouds, writing samples, etc.) as well as instructional interventions to meet the needs of and support learners? Do teachers have the opportunity to collaborate with their colleagues and share their problem-solving approaches to meet the range of students that they serve (Taylor, Pressley, and Pearson 2002)?

With DIBELS teachers are not able to be engaged professionally to use their judgments in a fashion that is discerning. Teachers are faced with a search for workbooks that teach, for example, nonsense words in a fashion akin to how DIBELS might test. Rather than identifying schoolwide efforts to help them use their professional judgment, teachers are responsible for DIBELS benchmarks but constrained from acting as professional teachers.

DIBELS represents a set of contradictions for teachers. On the one hand, DIBELS is claimed to be a tool for teachers to screen students, monitor their progress, and assess their achievements; on the other hand, that set of tools is limiting. We find ourselves questioning whether DIBELS supports effective teacher decision making or not. Does DIBELS define what teachers do in ways that may narrow rather than expand the tools that they might enlist, their understanding of student literacy development, and the range of practices that they might use to teach and assess students?

Discussion

In the name of improving literacy instruction, federal educational policy makers are enforcing mandates that impose practices and assessments such as DIBELS. While advocates of the National Reading Panel report tend to propose selected scripted approaches to teaching and learning, the panelists emphasized the important role played by nonscripted thinking by teachers if one hoped to improve learning. For example, in the NRP discussions of phonics and comprehension, stress was placed upon the teacher being strategic rather than scripted regardless of whether the goal was teaching phonics or comprehension. The NRP recommendation for phonics states:

> The role of the teacher needs to be better understood. Some of the phonics programs showing large effect sizes are scripted so that teacher judgment is largely eliminated. Although scripts may standardize instruction, they may reduce teachers' interest in the teaching process or their motivation to teach phonics. Thus, one concern is how to maintain consistency of instruction and at the same time encourage unique contributions from teachers. (2000, 2–135)

In discussing text comprehension, the NRP was more forthcoming about the role of the teacher:

> Strategic reading requires strategic teaching, which involves putting teachers in positions where their minds are their most valued educational resource. (2000, 4–49)

> The important development of instruction of comprehension research is the study of teacher preparation for instruction of multiple, flexible strategies in natural settings and content areas and the assessment of the effectiveness of this instruction by prepared teachers of comprehension. (4–52)

In discussing empowering teachers in conjunction with his NRC presidential address, Duffy suggested:

> Empowering teachers means creating the conditions in which teachers can make up their own minds, do their best work, and define their own context. (1990)

Duffy also quoted Bruce Burke:

> Do we do this? Do we invest in the minds of teachers? Do we help them make up their own minds, do their own best work, define their own context? Or do we invest in our theories, programs, and procedures in the expectation that teachers will compliantly follow? (1990)

DIBELS perpetuates what Olson lamented:

> [T]he search for programs that work betrays an undue fondness for control over both the teachers that use the programs and the children who are expected to learn from them. (2004, 26)

Or as McNeil observed in Texas:

> They tried to teacher-proof the curriculum with a checklist for teaching behaviors and the student minimum competency skills tests. By so doing, they have made schools exceedingly comfortable for mediocre teachers who like to teach routine lessons according to a standard sequence and format, who like working as deskilled laborers not having to think about their work. They made being a Texas public school teacher extremely uncomfortable for those who know their subjects well, who teach in ways that engage their students, who want their teaching to reflect their own continued learning. (2000, 187)

Certainly, it is difficult to imagine very many professions accepting what has been occurring in the name of educational reform in the area of literacy education. For example, the health sector would be enraged if concerns about health led to the imposition of policy from a limited review of selected research by a panel with certain predilections. It would be viewed as scandalous if the policy makers then enlisted these findings to require the use of screening devices directed at some possible indicators and treatments from such findings—especially if the providing of such products was not done competitively and a step removed from health matters. And it would be regarded as unconscionable if the worth of such interventions were measured as if improvements in health could be assessed by how well the treatment was implemented or by use of the screening devices. However, if they did accept such impositions, it would suggest a willingness to pursue health policy directed at some (not all) secondary indicators, biased toward certain providers and a net result where performance on the secondary indicators might improve, but health might not. If this became known, the providers would suggest that what they did was legal and the policy makers would suggest that they did so based upon the evidence that they had. They might also find it prudent to protect them by blaming others—for example, the health profession.

Likewise, it is doubtful that politicians would fully accept pronouncements that the literacy level of politicians seemed to have reached a dire point. Certainly they would reject any policy that imposed screening devices and practices with their own eligibility for reelection tied to such tests, especially if these policies emanated from a panel that systematically excluded some evidence. In other words, they would question who was on the panel and its biases, especially how they were defining political reading, what research was reviewed, and how it was reviewed. Further, they would question the rapid charge to initiate policy, as well as those insider groups that had been positioned to profit from noncompetitive contracts for screening devices and instructional material.

Unfortunately, the aforementioned parodies befit what has occurred in literacy and are perpetuated when assessments such as DIBELS are mandated and diminish literacy learning.

Final Words

The perception of declines in literacy and the arguable critique of child-centered approaches as responsible were perpetuated and used to justify unprecedented intrusions by the federal government. These intrusions ranged from determinations of what can count as evidence to the formulation of plans of action that linked to interventions and assessment approaches, such as DIBELS. They represent accountability models that have an appeal in the short run, but have strong negative impacts in the long term and systemically.

References

Clay, M. 1991. *Becoming Literate: The Construction of Inner Control.* Portsmouth, NH: Heinemann.

———. 1998. *By Different Paths to Common Outcomes.* Portland, ME: Stenhouse.

Duffy, J. 1990. *What Counts in Teacher Education? Dilemmas in Educating Empowered Teachers.* National Reading Conference Presidential address. Miami, FL.

House, E. 1991. "Evaluation and Social Justice: Where Are We?" In *Evaluation and Education at the Quarter Century*, edited by M. W. McLaughlin and D. C. Phillips. Chicago: National Society for the Study of Education.

Lewis, C., and B. Fabos. 2005. "Instant Messaging, Literacies, and Social Identities." *Reading Research Quarterly* 40 (4): 470–501.

McNeil, L. M. 2000. *Contradictions of School Reform: Educational Costs of Standardized Testing*. New York: Routledge.

National Reading Panel. 2000. *Teaching Children to Read: An Evidence-Based Assessment of the Scientific Research Literature on Reading and Its Implications for Reading Instruction. Report of the Subgroups*. Washington DC: U.S. Department of Health and Human Services, Public Health Service, National Institutes of Health and the National Institute of Child Health and Human Development.

Nichols, S. L., and D. C. Berliner. 2005. "The Inevitable Corruption of Indicators and Educators Through High-Stakes Testing." *Education Policy Studies* (March). Educational Policy Studies Laboratory. Educational Policy Research Unit. EPSL-0503101-EPRU.

Nichols, S. L., G. Glass, and D. Berliner. 2005. "High-Stakes Testing and Student Achievement: Problems from No Child Left Behind." *Education Policy Studies* (March). Educational Policy Studies Laboratory. Educational Policy Research Unit. EPSL0509-105-EPRU.

No Child Left Behind Act of 2001, Pub. L. No. 107-110, 115 Stat. 1425 (2002).

Olson, D. 2004. "The Triumph of Hope over Experience in the Search for What Works: A Response to Slavin." *Educational Researcher* 33 (1): 24–26.

Pearson, P. D. 2002. *Up the Down Staircase: The Role of Research in Policy and Practice*. International Reading Association, San Francisco

Taylor, B., M. Pressley, and P. D. Pearson. 2002. "Research-Supported Characteristics of Teachers and Schools That Promote Teaching Achievement." In *Teaching Reading. Effective Schools, Accomplished Teachers*, edited by B. Taylor, M. Pressley, and P. D. Pearson, (361–373). Mahwah, NJ: Lawrence Erlbaum.

How DIBELS Failed Alabama: A Research Report

SUSAN SEAY, PH.D. STUDENT
University of Alabama, Birmingham

*B*eginning with the 2003–2004 school year, the Alabama State Board of Education mandated that the Dynamic Indicators of Basic Early Literacy Skills (DIBELS) be administered to all students in grades K–2 throughout the state. The Stanford Achievement Test was mandated for students in grades 3–11. In mandating this test sequence, state education officials claimed that it allows early identification of students who may be experiencing reading difficulties and allows teachers to provide intensive intervention designed to bring those students up to grade level in reading before they take the high-stakes SAT 10 in third grade. (Morton 2004; Wong and Guthrie 2004).

Many researchers (Appleman and Thompson 2002; Gordon and Reese 1997; Ohanian 2001; Paris 2005; Pedulla 2003, William 2000) have expressed doubts about the usefulness of such assessments and concern about the widespread use of testing practices that offer a one-size-fits-all approach, infringe on instructional time, and contradict what many educators feel are effective assessments of the reading process. On the other hand, DIBELS authors and other educators and researchers (Good, Simmons, and Kame'enui 2001; Elliott, Lee, Tollefson 2001) claim that these measurements are useful indicators of performance on high-stakes assessments and are the most effective way to assure that students reach grade level proficiency in reading.

The purpose of this study was to examine statistical relationships that exist between the DIBELS Oral Reading Fluency

(ORF) subtest and the SAT 10 Reading Comprehension subtest. The three-year study involved students from a highly diverse Alabama school district. Two groups were studied because some schools used DIBELS in first through third grades and some used it only in second and third grades.

Because ethnicity, gender, and socioeconomic status have been shown to be important factors in explaining test score discrepancies among student populations, these variables were also statistically analyzed.

Key questions answered by the study include how the DIBELS Oral Reading Fluency scores are correlated with student scores on the third-grade SAT 10 Reading Comprehension subtest and once identified by DIBELS testing, if student reading scores improve to benchmark level as indicated by the DIBELS ORF. The subtest labeled Oral Reading Fluency in DIBELS is a test of how many words a child can read accurately from a passage in one minute. The term *fluency* in this context means speed and accuracy. Though DIBELS includes several other subtests that deal with letter names, initial sounds, phoneme segmentation, and nonsense words, these are considered by the DIBELS authors as stepping stones to reading connected text and ORF is the only test that involves reading connected text. Furthermore the authors claim that "in general, oral reading fluency provides one of the best measures of reading competence, including comprehension, for children in first through third grades."

Findings from this study indicate that the DIBELS ORF scores have only a moderate positive correlation with scores on the SAT 10. The grade 1 DIBELS ORF score predicts 36 percent of the variance in third-grade SAT 10 scores. That leaves 64 percent of the variance in test scores unaccounted for. Even in grade 3, the DIBELS ORF score predicts less than 50 percent of the variance in third-grade SAT 10 scores. Clearly, these numbers do not indicate that DIBELS ORF is a strong predictor of performance on the SAT 10. Statistically, one could obtain better results from the toss of a coin. Logically it appears more likely that improved reading comprehension produced more rapid and accurate word naming than vice versa.

Additional findings indicated that a sizeable percentage of students never got out of a risk category as measured by DIBELS ORF scores. The DIBELS assessments presume to determine which students are at risk for reading difficulties, allowing teachers to begin intervention strategies early. However, after being identified in first grade or second grade as needing reading intervention and receiving intensive intervention, which stresses reading fast and accurately, more than 23 percent of all students in Sample One and 36 percent of all students in Sample Two were still in a risk category through the end of the third-grade year. Student populations overrepresented in the group that failed to benchmark were males, students on free- and reduced-lunch status, and minority students.

This result is consistent with the latest National Assessment of Educational Progress (NAEP) findings. According to the 2005 NAEP results for the state of Alabama, the percentages of students scoring at or above the proficient level in reading at fourth grade has not significantly changed from results in 2003 or from results in 1992. For the student populations most in need of quality reading intervention—male students, students of poverty, and minority students—the gaps persist. Scores on the SAT 10 for these groups of students remain relatively low. Male students continued to score at the forty-third percentile in reading on the 2003 and 2005 SAT 10 test; students classified as in poverty scored at the thirtieth percentile for both years; Black students scored at the twenty-ninth percentile on the 2003 SAT 10 and moved up only one percentile rank to the thirtieth percentile on the 2005 SAT 10 test, not enough to meet the test of statistical significance.

Unfortunately, Alabama reading scores are stagnant. The expectations that state authorities had that DIBELS would improve reading achievement have not been fulfilled. It is time for them to look seriously at current assessments and instructional strategies that focus only on speed and accuracy and not on comprehension. A stopwatch should not be a perquisite for teaching children to read.

Instructional time and resources are being allocated to a test that is not providing the payback the state had hoped for. Interventions based on DIBELS skills are not working with the most vulnerable student populations and NAEP results indicate that this is true for the state as a whole as well. Early detection through the DIBELS assessment, and extensive practice on the DIBELS skills, is not moving students to grade level proficiency in reading.

DIBELS ORF assessment measures how fast and accurately students can call words from a particular passage of text. One problem with the assessment is that inferences are made from the results that determine the instruction offered to students. There have been many documented instances of teaching to the test and narrowing of the curriculum, even to the extent of DIBELS becoming essentially the reading curriculum (Jones et al. 1999; Madaus 1991; Stecher, Barron, Chun, and Ross 2000). Even with repeated practice, including students timing one another with stopwatches, an unacceptably high number of students are being left behind by this assessment and the resulting instructional approach to reading.

> **A note from the researcher**
>
> The most glaring problem I see with the DIBELS assessments is that they have become the goal of instruction. When I visit schools and talk to teachers about reading instruction, I am invariably told how DIBELS scores are progressing, not how students are progressing. I seldom encounter a student who does not know what his or her DIBELS score is and where it should be, as well as where others in the class stand in respect to DIBELS scores. Teachers relate their class scores on DIBELS and how they compare to other teachers in the school. They aren't talking about instruction and what works for struggling readers, they are talking about data and test scores. The goal of instruction has become raising DIBELS scores, not teaching students to read, and unfortunately the findings from this study are a testament to that goal.

At issue in the debate over the effectiveness and utility of the DIBELS ORF assessments is whether we are measuring what really matters in reading. Findings from this study suggest that testing students on how fast they can read is not leading students in this district to higher test scores, and is clearly not leading to meaningful reading. When speed becomes the goal of reading instruction, rather than meaning and purpose, students lose. If the goal for students is students who want to read and who can read to learn, then use of the DIBELS ORF is contrary to the goal.

References

Appleman, D., and M. J. Thompson. 2002. "Fighting the Toxic Education Status Quo." *English Education*, January, 34(2): 95–103.

Dynamic Indicators of Basic Early Literacy Skills. http://dibels.uoregon.edu/ (accessed March 13, 2005).

Elliott, J., S. W. Lee, and N. Tollefson. 2001. "A Reliability and Validity Study of the Dynamic Indicators of Basic Early Literacy Skills, Modified." *School Psychology Review* 30: 33–49.

Good, I., H. Roland, D. C. Simmons, and E. J. Kame'enui, 2001. "The Importance and Decision-Making Utility of a Continuum of Fluency-Based Indicators of Foundational Reading Skills for Third-Grade High-Stakes Outcomes." *Scientific Studies of Reading* 5: 257–288. Hillsdale, NJ: Lawrence Erlbaum.

Gordon, S. P., and M. Reese. 1997. "High-Stakes Testing: Worth the Price?" *Journal of School Leadership* 7 (4): 345–368.

Jones, M., B. Jones, B. Hardin, L. Chapman, T. Yarbrough, and M. Davis. 1999. "The Impact of High-Stakes Testing on Teachers and Students in North Carolina." *Phi Delta Kappan* 81 (3): 199–203.

Kohn, A. 2002. "On Standardized Tests and Teachers." *English Education* 34: 95–103.

Madaus, G. 1991. "The Influence of Testing on the Curriculum." In *Critical Issues in Curriculum*, edited by L. Tanner, 83–121. Chicago: University of Chicago Press.

Morton, J. 2004. Personal communication, 14 July.

National Center for Education Statistics. 2005. "National Assessment of Educational Progress: The Nation's Report Card: State Profiles." http://nces.ed.gov/nationsreportcard/states/profile.asp (accessed October 15, 2005).

Ohanian, S. 2001. "News from the Test Resistance Trail." *Phi Delta Kappan* 82 (5): 363–366.

Paris, S. 2005. "Reinterpreting the Development of Reading Skills." *Reading Research Quarterly* 40 (2): 164–202.

Pedulla, J. J. 2003. "State-Mandated Testing: What Do Teachers Think?" *Educational Leadership* 61 (3): 42–46.

Stecher, B., S. Barron, T. Chun, and K. Ross. 2000. "The Effects of the Washington State Education Reform on Schools and Classrooms." CSE Tech. Rep. 525. Los Angeles: National Center for Research on Evaluation.

William, D. 2000. "The Meanings and Consequences of Educational Assessments." *Critical Quarterly* 42 (1): 105–127.

Wong, K., and J. Guthrie. 2004. *Alabama Educational Policy Primer*. Nashville, TN: Peabody Center for Education Policy, Vanderbilt University.

But Isn't DIBELS Scientifically Based?

SANDRA WILDE

*I*t suddenly seems as though DIBELS testing is everywhere; in fact, it seems to have replaced other assessments of reading in many school districts, particularly those receiving Reading First grants. Those who endorse the use of DIBELS say that one of the program's strong points is that the tests are an accurate predictor of potential reading failure—indeed, teachers have reported to me that this is what they are told in DIBELS workshops. The implication is that even if the DIBELS procedures seem unconnected to what real reading looks like, they're valuable in providing a quick screening tool for identifying which students need extra help.

I recently decided to put this claim to the test. I examined the findings from two studies linked to on DIBELS's own website at the University of Oregon. Since these studies have been made available by the program itself, I assumed they would offer a best-case scenario of how strong a predictor DIBELS is. Both studies deal with the Oral Reading Fluency subtest (see the Appendix), the subtest most often used and indeed the only one offered in grades 2–6.

First, I looked at a study by Buck and Torgesen (2003), which aimed to find out "whether performance on brief, one-minute measures of oral reading fluency are predictive of achievement in reading as measured by the reading portion of the [Florida state assessment]." The students were categorized by the DIBELS Oral Reading Fluency subtest (ORF), which measures the number of words read correctly in one minute, into three groups: high, some, or low risk. Each of these groups was then divided into two sub-

Table 1: *Buck and Torgesen Study Data*

| | Words correct per minute | | | |
	High Risk: <80	Some Risk: 80–109	Low Risk: >110	Totals
Adequate *(Meeting State Benchmark)*	42	188	511	741 (67%)
Inadequate *(Not Meeting State Benchmark)*	178	130	53	361 (33%)
Number and *Percent of Total*	220 (20%)	318 (29%)	564 (51%)	1102

Sensitivity = .77
Specificity = .92
(Calculated only for the high-risk and low-risk groups)

groups, those who did and didn't meet the state benchmark in reading. The DIBELS tests were conducted a month after the state tests, so what's being measured is not so much prediction of a future test score but correlation with a current one, which statistically amounts to pretty much the same thing. The results appear in Table 1.

At first glance, it seems that the DIBELS test was a pretty good predictor. After all, students who scored as low-risk on it were likely to meet the state standard, while high-risk students were not. However, let's think about what the numbers might mean for actual classroom practice.

If this DIBELS test were used to decide which students should receive extra instruction, schools would have to determine whether to help just the high-risk students or the some-risk ones as well. There were 361 students who didn't meet the state benchmark; only half of them (178) would have gotten extra help if it only went to those in the high-risk category. If help were given to the high-risk and some-risk categories, it would catch most of those likely to not meet benchmark (308), but extra help would also be given to 230 students who didn't need it. Indeed, the high- and some-risk groups combined make up nearly 50 percent of the study's population.

Table 2: *Wilson Study Data*

	High Risk	**Some Risk**	**Low Risk**
Meeting State Standard	7.0%	51.4%	81.9%
Not Meeting State Standard	93.0%	48.6%	18.1%

Let's look at another study, this one from Arizona (Wilson 2005). The tests were also given to third graders, in this case 241 of them. The study didn't indicate how many students fell into each subgroup, so their results, in Table 2, appear as percentages only. (48 percent of the students passed the state test.)

Again, the prediction is strong only if you leave out the "some risk" group; half the students in this group passed the state assessment and half didn't, so the DIBELS test had no predictive value at all for them. One would again be in a situation of providing extra help to students who didn't need it or missing those who did.

What conclusions do the authors of these studies draw? According to Buck and Torgesen, "This initial study demonstrates that, for a large heterogeneous group of third graders, performance on brief oral reading fluency measures can quite accurately predict whether or not a given student will attain a [passing score on the Florida] reading test" (2003, 9). Well, no. Only those who score in the high-risk or low-risk group, which of course include the strongest and weakest of readers, those whose teachers already know if they're likely to pass the state test. Interestingly, Buck and Torgesen chose to leave out the some-risk group in calculating sensitivity and specificity scores—roughly, how likely the results are to be accurate: the true positive and true negative, respectively. The test isn't really predictive at all for the middle, some-risk group.

Wilson's conclusions are also problematic. It may be reasonable to say, as he does, that "ORF can identify those students who are likely to meet the proficiency standard on [the state test] with good accuracy" (i.e., 82 percent), but it's not true that it can "identify those who are quite unlikely to reach proficiency" (2005, 4).

Again, no. Not unless you also include quite a few students who don't need help.

So much for the vaunted claims that a one-minute read-aloud is all that you need to identify who needs extra help with reading. I've only looked at two studies here, but is it likely that other studies would show dramatically different results? Although many schools use DIBELS as an initial prescreen to be followed by other assessment, Oregon teacher Donna Shrier (personal communication 2006) informed me that in her district, the DIBELS oral reading score determines whether students are in Title I programs and what kind of instruction they get. Teachers are required to provide any student who performs at the high-risk level with intensive instruction that is heavily phonics-based, "because that's the only way these kids can learn." Another teacher in the district told me that a student of hers who performed at the benchmark level on DIBELS (i.e, in the low-risk range) was removed from Title I instruction even though she hadn't passed the state test and, in the teacher's opinion, needed extra help. When I asked her what the district office would say if asked the rationale for this policy, she replied, "They'd say it's scientifically based."

Well, maybe this scientific emperor has no clothes, or skimpy ones at best. The DIBELS website supports the Oral Reading Fluency subtest by saying that eight studies in the 1980s found criterion-related validity of the test (usually determined by comparing a measure with other tests) to range from .52 to .91 (dibels.uoregon.edu/measures/orf2.php), hardly a stunning performance when it comes to making decisions about individual students, especially upon taking a closer look at the numbers as I've done for the two studies described.

And it's the effect on individual students that really matters here. It would be one thing to use DIBELS to predict, for instance, what proportion of students in a school are likely to fail the state reading test, but it's clearly not that good at identifying *which* students they'll be. Also, if DIBELS were used as a quick initial screen to identify which students need further assessment, that would be reasonable (although it would still miss some cases), but it often drives out other forms of assessment that would be far more sensitive to a variety of reading problems. The hard sell of DIBELS promotional efforts, with a strong veneer of being "scientifically based," has had a powerful effect on educational decision makers.

I haven't even tried to touch on the larger issues, such as whether state reading tests are a good measure of reading competence, let alone what kind of instruction best benefits struggling readers. But DIBELS fails on the most basic grounds of validity; that is, whether it measures what it claims to be measuring. As Kenneth Goodman stated earlier in this volume, scores on reading tests tend to correlate highly with each other no matter what. But the DIBELS Oral Reading Fluency subtest claims to do something more: to strongly predict whether individual children are likely to fail to learn to read. It just doesn't.

References

Buck, J., and J. Torgesen. 2003. *The Relationship Between Performance on a Measure of Oral Reading Fluency and Performance on the Florida Comprehensive Assessment Test*. FCRR Technical Report #1. Tallahassee, FL: Florida Center for Reading Research. dibels.uoregon.edu/techreports/index.php.

Wilson, J. 2005. *The Relationship of Dynamic Indicators of Basic Early Literacy Skills (DIBELS) Oral Reading Fluency to Performance on Arizona Instrument to Measure Standards (AIMS)*. Tempe, AZ: Tempe School District, Assessment and Evaluation Department. dibels.uoregon.edu/techreports/index.php.

DIBELS: Not Justifiable*

MARYANN MANNING, CONSTANCE KAMII,
and TSUGUHIKO KATO
University of Alabama at Birmingham

Since the Reading Excellence Act, Alabama has had a program called the Alabama Reading Initiative. Although initially the Alabama Reading Initiative used several reading assessments, under pressure from the federal No Child Left Behind (NCLB) proposal reviewers, the Dynamic Indicators of Basic Early Literacy Skills (DIBELS) (Good and Kaminski 2002) was chosen to evaluate the Reading First grant. But Alabama and several other states have gone beyond NCLB mandates and require that all public schools administer DIBELS to all students in kindergarten through third grade.

We decided to investigate the value of two DIBELS subtests used in first grade: Phoneme Segmentation Fluency (PSF) and Nonsense Word Fluency (NWF). Phoneme Segmentation Fluency (PSF) is a test of students' ability to segment three- and four-phoneme words into their individual phonemes. For example, if the examiner says "sat," the student has to say "/s/ /a/ /t/" to receive three possible points. The number of correct phonemes produced in one minute is the child's score. Nonsense Word Fluency (NWF) is a decoding test. For example, when the written *vaj* is presented, the student has to say "/v/ /a/ /j/" or "vaj" to receive full credit. The child's score is the number of letter-sounds produced correctly in one minute. Many teachers have reported

---

*This chapter is based on "Dynamic Indicators of Basic Early Literacy Skills (DIBELS): A Tool for Evaluating Student Learning?" *Journal of Research in Childhood Education* 20 (2): 81–96.

that students get low scores on the one-minute DIBELS Nonsense Word Fluency subtest when they take a long time trying to make sense of each "make-believe" word such as *fob* and *suv*. The authors of DIBELS state that "the PSF measure has been found to be a good predictor of later reading achievement (Good and Kaminski 2002, 16), and we wanted to know if this test also correlated with current achievement in reading and writing.

We analyzed the January scores of 101 first graders attending a public school in a small Southern town on the two DIBELS subtests as well as two other assessments. The 101 students had been heterogeneously assigned to seven classrooms. Six of the seven teachers' instruction included exercises in phonemic segmentation and isolated phonics. The children were 95 percent Caucasian, 4 percent African American, and 1 percent Asian American.

Within one or two weeks of the administration of the DIBELS, we gave each child an individual Slosson Oral Reading Test and a writing test that we had developed. The Slosson is a test of ability to read single real words. We used the Slosson score of the total number of words read correctly.

In our writing task, we asked each child to write four pairs of words on a blank sheet of paper—*ham* and *hamster*, *butter* and *butterfly*, *melon* and *watermelon*, and *berry* and *strawberry*. These words were selected because the second word of each pair was longer and included the same sounds that were in the first word and permitted the identification of thirteen levels of development (Kamii and Manning 1999) ranging from random strings of letters with no apparent relationship to the intended oral word (Level 1) to invented spellings easily read by anyone who can read English (Level 5). The middle levels represent increasing approximations of the intended words. At Level 2YD, for example (see Figure 1), the child wrote *elgPS* for *ham* and *elgPSSAWiS* for *hamster*, using the same letters unconventionally for *ham* and the beginning of *hamster*. He likewise wrote *BigSUMLE* for *butter* and the beginning of *butterfly*. At Level 3YC (see Figure 2), the child wrote the same letters conventionally at the beginning of *ham* and *hamster* and *butter* and *butterfly*. She also wrote the same letters for *melon* and the end of *watermelon*.

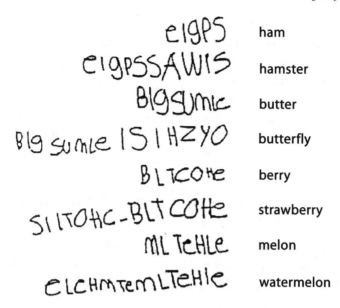

eIgPS	ham
eIgPSSAWIS	hamster
BIgSumlc	butter
BIg sumle ISIHZYO	butterfly
BLTCOte	berry
SIITOHC-BLTCOtte	strawberry
MLTeHLe	melon
eLCHmTemLTeHIe	watermelon

Figure 1: *An Example of Level 2YD Writing*

Hmy	ham
HSDr	hamster
BDr	butter
BDrFLY	butterfly
maLn	berry
WDrmaLn	strawberry
Bye	melon
hBc	watermelon

Figure 2: An Example of Level 3YC Writing

73

We gave the Slosson Oral Reading Test because it presents real words for children to read rather than nonsense words like *vaj* and *fob*. The Slosson gave us of the number of real words a first grader could read as compared to the DIBELS Nonsense Word Fluency subtest. Our writing task was given because the writing gives us information about the child's developing ideas about the nature of our writing system. We hypothesized that the DIBELS should give us similar information.

Findings About DIBELS Phoneme Segmentation Fluency (PSF)

If Phonemic Segmentation Fluency is useful in sounding out real words, a high correlation can be expected between the scores on the Slosson and PSF. However, the correlation we found was only .07 (close to none).

Table 1 shows the relationship between PSF and the levels found with our writing test. If phonemic segmentation is important in writing, there should be a high correlation between per-

Table 1: *Relationship Between DIBELS Phonemic Segmentation Fluency (PSF, in Percentiles) and Level of Writing in First Grade*

| | DIBELS PSF (Percentiles) | | | | | |
	1–20	21–40	41–60	61–80	81–100	(Total)
Level of Writing						
0 and 1	1					(1)
2	3	0	1			(4)
2Y, 2YA, 2YB, 2YC, and 2YD	0	1				(1)
3YA and 3YB	2	2	1	2	1	(8)
3YC and 3YD	10	25	18	16	9	(78)
4	1	2	1	1	2	(7)
5	1	0	1			(2)
(Total)	(18)	(30)	(22)	(19)	(12)	(101)

Somers' d = .10 (n.s.)

formance on the PSF and the writing test. But our first graders scored slightly more frequently toward the lower end of the PSF distribution; yet 87 percent (78 percent + 7 percent + 2 percent at Levels 3YC, 3YD, 4, and 5) were writing with at least some invented spelling. The great majority of those writing at relatively high levels are distributed across the entire range of PSF scores, and there are as many low-PSF cases (21–40 percentile) as high-PSF cases (61–100 percentile) writing words at a relatively high level. So it is possible to write words at a relatively high level without being able to sound out words on the DIBELS PSF.

Findings About DIBELS Nonsense Word Fluency (NWF)

The correlation between NWF and the Slosson was statistically significant, but we can see in Table 2 that many children with low NWF scores (1–40 percentile) wrote words at relatively high levels (Levels 3YC, 3YD, and 4).

Table 2: *Relationship between DIBELS Nonsense Word Fluency (Percentiles) and Level of Writing in First Grade*

	DIBELS NWF (Percentiles)					
	1–20	**21–40**	**41–60**	**61–80**	**81–100**	**(Total)**
Level of Writing						
0 and 1	1					(1)
2	4					(4)
2Y, 2YA, 2YB, 2YC, and 2YD	0					(0)
3YA and 3YB	1	2	3	1	1	(8)
3YC and 3YD	9	12	21	22	15	(78)
4	0	1	0	4	2	(7)
5					2	(2)
(Total)	(15)	(15)	(24)	(27)	(20)	(101)

Somers' d = .10 (n.s.)

Relationships Among Scores on Some DIBELS Subtests

The correlation between the Phonemic Segmentation Fluency (PSF) and Nonsense Word Fluency (NWF) was found to be a low .29 (p <.01), indicating some relationship between the ability to segment spoken words phonemically and the ability to decode written nonsense. It would be surprising if there were no relationship. The low correlation suggests the tests are not of equal difficulty and success on one does not predict the success on the other the DIBELS authors claim it does.

Because the schools provided scores on the DIBELS Oral Reading Fluency (ORF) subtest, we decided to find out how these scores related to PSF and NWF. Oral Reading Fluency is a subtest of the number of words read correctly per minute by a child reading a passage. The correlation was .13 (not significant statistically) between Oral Reading Fluency and Phonemic Segmentation Fluency. So the score for sounding out real words has no relationship to the number of words read correctly in a real passage. Again the authors' claim that the PSF score would predict success in correct reading of real words in a passage was not supported.

Between Oral Reading Fluency and Nonsense Word Fluency, the correlation was .70 (p < .01). It is not surprising that children who can read words correctly also do better on reading nonsense syllables, but that does not mean that the ability to read nonsense precedes the ability to read sensible text. Furthermore, the score on the ORF is the number of words read correctly and does not require the reader to make sense of the passage.

The low correlations found between Phoneme Segmentation Fluency and everything else strongly suggest that the utility of DIBELS PSF must be questioned.

As for Nonsense Word Fluency, it correlated moderately with the Slosson word recognition test and with DIBELS Oral Reading Fluency. But it was low with our writing test probably because the scoring of the Nonsense Word Fluency test penalizes students who try to make sense of the nonsense.

Conclusion

The question that must now be answered is: Is the use of the DIBELS justifiable? As the name Dynamic Indicators of Basic Early Literacy Skills (DIBELS) denotes, the subtests are based on the theory that reading and writing consist of skills such as phonemic segmentation and decoding. By contrast, our writing task is based on the theory that reading and writing involve children's knowledge of our writing system, which each child constructs by going through one level after another of being "wrong." We strongly disagree with the view that reading and writing are mere collections of skills.

Our writing task yields much more information than PSF and NWF for the same amount of testing time. In every word a child writes (such as *HM* for *ham*), his or her level of phonemic segmentation as well as of graphophonic information is evident. Our writing task also gives information about the child's knowledge before invented spelling, such as whether or not the child thinks that writing is related to speaking. Our confidence in our writing task comes in part from a longitudinal study (Kamii, Long, and Manning 2001).

DIBELS is based on an outdated, limited scientific theory, and the evidence provided by the present study does not justify its use for the evaluation of an instructional program. Each successive subtest is not a good predictor of success on the next subtest, and none of the tests we examined show much relationship to real reading or writing.

References

Good, R. H., and R. A. Kaminski, eds. 2002. *Dynamic Indicators of Basic Early Literacy Skills.* 6th edition. Eugene, OR: Institute for the Development of Educational Achievement. http://dibels.uoregon.edu/.

Kamii, C., R. Long, and M. Manning. 2001. "Kindergartners' Development Toward Invented Spelling and a Glottographic Theory." *Linguistics and Education* 12 (2): 195–210.

Kamii, C., and M. Manning. 1999. "Before Invented Spelling: Kindergartners' Awareness That Writing Is Related to the Sounds of Speech." *Journal of Research in Childhood Education* 14 (1): 16–25.

Appendix: A Brief Summary of Each Subtest in DIBELS

Letter Naming Fluency (LNF)*

This is to be administered on all three kindergarten testings and in beginning first grade. Alternate forms are provided for each testing.

The task in this subtest is to name as many letters shown in a mixed line of lower- and uppercase letters as possible in one minute. The tester says, "Tell me the names of as many letters as you can. Start here [point to first letter] and go across the page. Point to each letter and tell me the name of that letter." If the child responds with a sound the tester is told to say, "Tell me the name, not the sound it makes" once and only once and to count any subsequent sound responses as wrong.

A stopwatch is used. That's also true in all other subtests. The tester puts a slash through each wrong letter on a scoring sheet. If a child does not name a letter in three seconds the tester says the name of the letter and says "What letter?", pointing to the next letter. The test ends after one minute, or after the first ten letters not correctly named.

The authors indicate that although the test does not relate to one of the Big Ideas and "does not appear to be essential to achieve reading outcomes," the lowest 20 percent in the school district should be considered at risk, and between 20 to 40 percent at some risk. This deviates from other subtests that have benchmarks of specific scores to be achieved at each level.

---

*At times in the manual the subtest acronyms have a *D* in front of them (i.e., DLNF) and at times they do not.

This test is the first one in the teachers' manual but follows the Initial Sound Fluency in the pupil materials so it is unclear what sequence is intended.

The instructions and scoring examples allow the tester to count articulation and dialect variations as correct. Examples are provided, for example, "thee for see or eth for ess," but no dialect examples are given. They are told to use "professional judgment" in doing so. But the rating sheet provided for training testers does not evaluate their ability to do this. And no special training is provided for making such judgments. This is a serious issue that bears on whether DIBELS scores are in fact equivalent across testers and across populations of children.

Initial Sound Fluency (ISF)

This test is actually recommended for preschool through middle kindergarten and "for monitoring progress of older children with very low skills in phonological awareness."

The examiner shows four pictures to the child and names each of them with a word orally. The examiner says one word begins with its initial sound (i.e., *mouse* starts with /m/) and then asks the child to point out the picture that starts with another sound. The child's task is to point to the picture that "begins with the sound." In each set of four pictures the child is also asked once, "What sound does _____ (a picture name) start with?"

The child has five seconds to respond. The child is permitted to answer all questions but the time taken is noted on the stopwatch and the score is the number of correct responses per minute. The test is discontinued after five missed questions.

For this test the benchmark is twenty-five to thirty-five initial sounds right in mid-kindergarten. Fewer than ten sounds "may need intensive instructional support." The test is not administered in the third kindergarten testing.

The tester may count correct variations in articulation and pronunciation. But a single pronunciation guide is provided, and again the ability to make such judgments is not part of the evaluation of the testers.

Phoneme Segmentation Fluency (PSF)

Intended for Use from Mid-Kindergarten Through All Three First-Grade Testings

This is also intended as a test of phonological awareness. It's an oral test in which the tester says a three- or four-phoneme word and the pupil must produce the separate phonemes fluently (that is, fast and accurately.)

The tester says: "I am going to say a word. After I say it, you tell me all the sounds in the word." The child has three seconds to do so, after which a zero is scored and the tester goes on. The tester underlines each correct sound and puts a slash through the wrong ones. The test stops in one minute and one point is given for each correct segment. If five words are missed the test is stopped.

Again dialect and articulation variation may be counted correct although a single pronunciation chart is provided.

The benchmark for Spring of kindergarten and Fall of first grade is thirty-five to forty-five correct and fewer than ten is needing intense instruction.

Nonsense Word Fluency (NWF)

Required for Mid-Kindergarten Through First Grade

The intent of this subtest is to measure the "alphabetic principle." The child has a letter-sized sheet of paper with rows of random CVC tri-graphs or VC di-graphs which the child is told are "make-believe" words. *b*, *w*, *y*, and *r* are used only in initial positions. *c* and *g* are used only in final positions. *x* and *q* are not used.

The task is to either produce a correct sound for each letter or say the whole "word" correctly. In either case each correct sound gets a point. The authors say they are aware that by producing words the child can get more points in a minute than by matching sounds to letters.

If the child does not try in three seconds and is responding sound by sound, the tester marks the sound wrong, points to the next letter and says, "What sound?" If the child is responding word by word the examiner points to the next word and says, "What word?"

The benchmark is fifty correct "letter sounds" in one minute by mid-first grade. Fewer than thirty may need intensive instruction. Articulation or dialect variations may be counted, although a single pronunciation guide is provided.

Oral Reading Fluency (ORF)

Required for "Most Children from Mid-First Grade Through Third Grade"

The intent is to test "accuracy and fluency with connected text." Although connected text is not defined it may be assumed that the passages provided in DIBELS are exemplars of what the authors mean by that. The manual claims that the passages are "calibrated for the goal level of reading for each grade level." That should mean they've taken some pains to assure that the passages are not too hard or too easy for the children being tested in each grade. But they do not indicate in the manual how they were calibrated. Teachers report that the passages are difficult for their students. Every passage is one page in length and for all three grades each is a first person narrative, more like a child's composition than a story. Each appears to have a theme but no plot. There is a single passage each in second and third grade that has a nature theme. No explanation is provided for these choices.

The child's task is to read a given passage aloud for one minute. Omitted or incorrect words are counted wrong. The tester marks each incorrect word and tells the reader the next word after three seconds. The score is the number of words read correctly in one minute. Self-corrections within three seconds are counted as correct.

If the reader gets more than ten words right in a minute, then he or she is asked to read a second and third passage each allowing one minute. The middle score is counted if all three are read. Benchmarked passages are provided for each level.

ORF Retell Fluency

This subtest is administered following each ORF passage reading (if ten words are read correctly), although it is scored separately. In stating the purpose of this subtest the authors say:

> Retell Fluency (RTF) is intended to provide a comprehension check for the DORF assessment. In general, oral reading fluency provides one of the best measures of reading competence, including comprehension, for children in first through third grades. The purpose of the RTF measure is to (a) prevent inadvertently learning or practicing a misrule, (b) identify children whose comprehension is not consistent with their fluency, (c) provide an explicit linkage to the core components in the NRP report, and (d) increase the face validity of the DORF.

The authors seem to consider the retelling an unnecessary add-on since they believe Oral Reading Fluency is itself an adequate measure of competence, including comprehension. That equates word accuracy with comprehension since that's what is scored in ORF.

The "misrule" that the authors are concerned about is:

> that speed-reading without attending to meaning is either desirable or the intent of the oral reading fluency measure. With a prompted retell, children will be less likely to conclude that simply reading as fast as they can is the desired behavior, and teachers will be less likely to imply that simply reading as fast as they can is desired.

The authors say the retelling measure has been added because:

> Teachers frequently are concerned about children who read fluently and do not comprehend. My [sic] read of the data is that this pattern is infrequent—but may apply to some children. It seems to me [sic] this procedure may identify those children without increasing unduly the amount of time spent in the assessment.

DIBELS claims it deals with the first three Big Ideas of the National Reading Panel. The Oral Reading Fluency measure, according to the authors, "corresponds directly to the comprehension core component. The current oral reading fluency measure corresponds about as well as anything to reading comprehension. Retell Fluency provides an additional, explicit score."

To begin the Retelling Fluency, the tester says, "Please tell me all about what you just read. Try to tell me everything you can. Begin." If a child pauses for three seconds the tester prompts once and only once: "Try to tell me everything you can." The score is the number of words in the retelling in one minute not counting repetitions or "getting off track."

Word Use Fluency (WUF)

Recommended for Use from Kindergarten Through Third Grade

The tester is provided with a single list of eighteen random words for each grade from K–3. No information is provided on how they are chosen. Most are nouns, verbs, or words that can be used as either.

The tester provides two examples and says, "Listen to me use a word." Then the tester says, "Your turn to use the word."

Then the tester says, "OK, here is your word." The child has five seconds to "use" the word correctly in a "phrase, expression, definition, or sentence." After five seconds, the next word is said by the tester.

The score is the number of words in each correct "utterance" that use the target words in a total of one minute. "Utterances are scored liberally" if they either involve correct use or correct definition. If the first five words are not used correctly the test is discontinued.

The authors state:

> A benchmark goal is not provided for WUF because additional research is needed to establish its linkage to other big ideas of early literacy. . . . Tentatively, students in the lowest 20 percent of a school district using local norms should be considered at risk for poor language and reading outcomes, and those between the

20th percentile and 40th percentile should be considered at some risk.

That appears to make this test optional but it is unclear why these criteria have been set for it. Perhaps the testers believe they are testing vocabulary but they do not say so in the manual.

Contributors

Ken Goodman is Professor Emeritus of Language, Reading, and Culture at the University of Arizona.

Alan Flurkey is Director of the Reading/Writing Learning Clinic and a member of the faculty of the Literacy Studies Department in the School of Education and Allied Human Services at Hofstra University.

Constance Kamii is Professor of Education at the University of Alabama at Birmingham.

Tsuguhiko Kato is a doctoral student and graduate assistant in early childhood education at the University of Alabama at Birmingham.

Lisa Laser is a homeschooling parent in Joseph, Oregon.

Maryann Manning is Professor of Education at the University of Alabama at Birmingham.

P. David Pearson is Dean of the College of Education at the University of California, Berkeley.

Susan Seay is operations director of Better Basics, Inc., a nonprofit that provides reading support services to children in Birmingham, Alabama.

Catherine Thome is Language Arts Coordinator and Reading First Grant Director for Lake County Regional Office of Education, Greyslake, Illinois.

Robert J. Tierney is Dean of the Faculty of Education and Professor of Language and Literacy at the University of British Columbia, Vancouver.